KNITTING stylish STITCHES

Lyric Books Limited

© 1993 Lyric Books Limited,
66B The Broadway, Mill Hill, London NW7 3TF, England
First published in 1993
ISBN 0 7111 0082 9
Printed in Belgium by Proost International Book Production

Series Consultant: Eleanor Van Zandt

Art Editor: Stefanie Paradine
Graphics: Pauline Moss, Jacqueline Kanareck
Production Editor: Monika York
Production Assistant: Jenny Mc Ivor

CONTENTS

Introduction — 4
Shaping — 5
Types of Knitting — 8
Garment Styles and Features — 14
Making Up — 17
Abbreviations — 19

Woman's Waistcoat — 22
Lace Patterns — 26
Lace Panels — 28

His and Her Guernsey Sweater — 30
Knit and Purl Textures — 34
Knit and Purl Patterns — 36
Knit and Purl Panels — 37

Cabled Dress — 40
Rib Patterns — 43
Cable Panels — 46
Cable Patterns — 52

Man's Cardigan — 55
Intarsia Motifs — 60

Fair Isle Top — 65
Fair Isle Patterns — 69

Child's Sailor Cardigan — 74
Rich Textures — 78
Raised Stitches — 80

Introduction

STYLISH STITCHES is for the knitter who has mastered the basic skills presented in STARTING STITCHES and wants to progress to more ambitious projects. In these pages you will learn the techniques of decorative increasing and decreasing, which are required for many interesting stitch patterns, including knitted lace. The more advanced cable techniques are presented, along with the two main methods of colour-patterned knitting: Fair Isle, or stranded knitting and intarsia, or motif knitting.

You will also learn various construction methods, including working in the round on circular or double-pointed needles and working bands and borders. And to help you give your garments a truly professional finish, we show you how to join pieces with a neat mattress stitch seam.

The six projects include a waistcoat with cable panels, a Guernsey-style sweater for men and women, a dress with a cabled yoke, worked in the round, a man's cardigan with a bold intarsia pattern, a toddler's cardigan with a Fair Isle motif and a cool, sophisticated Fair Isle pullover in delicious pastel colours.

Each project is accompanied by a selection of related stitch patterns and colour motifs, which we hope will inspire you to do a little experimenting.

The Editors

Shaping

SHAPING

In addition to the simple decreasing and increasing techniques covered in STARTING STITCHES, there are a number of slightly more complex shaping methods required for various shapes and stitch patterns.

Left-sloping decrease

If you knit two stitches together in the ordinary way (k2tog, p2tog; STARTING STITCHES, page 16), the decreased stitches slope to the right. This does not matter if a simple edge decrease is required but there are times when the effect will be visible, and you will need to decrease in a given direction, to the right or to the left. As used here, the terms 'right' and 'left' refer to the direction as the row being worked is facing you and not necessarily the direction on the right side of the work.

On a knit row there are three basic ways of creating a slope to the left.

Knit row - Method 1

1. Slip the first stitch knitwise on to the right-hand needle, then knit the next stitch.

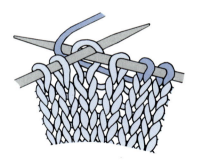

2. Using the left-hand needle, lift the slipped stitch over the knitted stitch and off the needle. This is call 'slip one, knit one, pass slipped stitch over' (**sl 1, k1, psso,** or in some patterns, **skpo**).

Knit row - Method 2

This is worked in a similar way to k2tog but the stitches are knitted through the back of the loops.

Insert the right-hand needle from right to left through the back of the first two stitches, then knit them together as one stitch. This is called 'knit two together through back of loops' (**k2togtbl**).

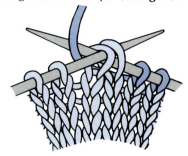

Knit row - Method 3

Slip the first and second stitches knitwise one at a time on to the right-hand needle, then insert the left-hand needle through the fronts of these two stitches and knit them together from this position. This is called 'slip, slip, knit' (**ssk**).

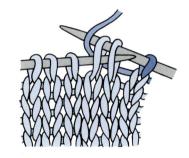

Purl row

There is only one way to achieve a slope to the left (on the right side) while working a purl row and that is to purl two stitches together through the back of the loops - a slightly awkward manoeuvre.

From the back insert the right-hand needle from left to right through the back of the second stitch, then the first, twisting them as shown. Then purl them together as one stitch. This is called 'purl two together through back of loops' (**p2togtbl**).

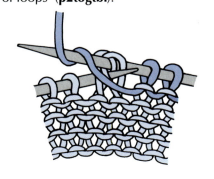

Decreasing two stitches

It is often necessary to decrease two stitches at the same point. The following methods are generally worked on right side rows and all create different effects.

To create a slope towards the left work as follows:

1. Slip the first stitch on to the right-hand needle, then knit the next two stitches together.

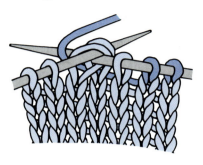

2. Lift the slipped stitch over the new stitch and off the needle. This is called 'slip one, knit two together, pass slipped stitch over' (**sl 1, k2tog, psso**).

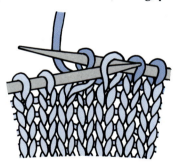

To create a slope towards the right insert the needle knitwise into the first three stitches and knit them together as one stitch. This is called 'knit three together' (**k3tog**).

For a vertical decrease (where the centre stitch remains central) work to one stitch before the centre stitch and continue as follows:

Shaping

1. Insert the right-hand needle knitwise into the first two stitches as if to k2tog, then slip them on to the right-hand needle.

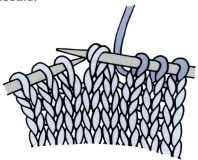

2. Knit the next stitch, then lift the two slipped stitches over the knit stitch and off the needle. This is called 'slip two together, knit one, pass two slipped stitches over' (**sl 2tog, k1, p2sso**).

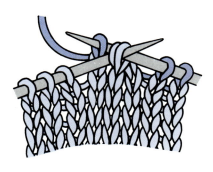

On a purl row the most usual method of decreasing two stitches is to work to one stitch before the centre stitch, then purl three together (**p3tog**). Work this in the same way as p2tog but insert the needle through three stitches instead of two.

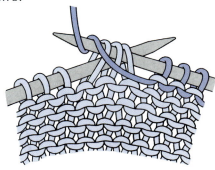

Fully fashioning

Raglan armhole shaping is often 'fully fashioned'. This means that the decreases are worked one or more stitches in from the edge of the work and slant to the right or left according to the direction of the raglan slope. This leaves a neat edge for seaming and enhances the raglan shape. Raglan seams should be joined matching row for row before the side and sleeve seams are joined.

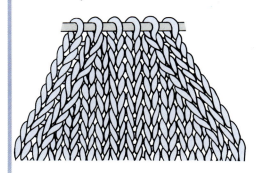

Eyelet methods of increasing

Another method of increasing is to make an extra loop between two stitches. This loop is then knitted or purled on the next row. This technique forms a hole in the material and is used as a decorative feature, especially in lace patterns.

An eyelet increase is sometimes called a 'yarn over' increase and in American patterns (and some British ones) it is abbreviated simply 'yo'. In traditional British pattern terminology, however, a distinction is made according to the type of stitch preceding and following the increase. In all cases, however, the yarn travels in the same direction: up in front of the needle, then over it.

A hole between two knit stitches
Bring the yarn forward as if to purl a stitch but then knit the next stitch, taking the yarn over the needle in order to do so. This is called 'yarn forward' (**yf** or **yfwd**).

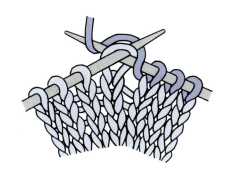

A hole between two purl stitches
Take the yarn over the top of the needle, then between the needles to

Shaping

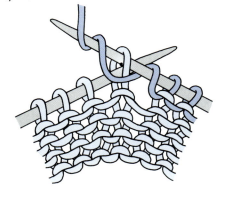

A hole between a knit and a purl stitch
Bring the yarn forward as if to purl, then over the needle to the back, then between the needles to the front again before purling the next stitch. This is called 'yarn over needle' (**yon**).

the front again before purling the next stitch. This is called 'yarn forward and round needle' (**yfrn** or in some patterns, **yrn**).

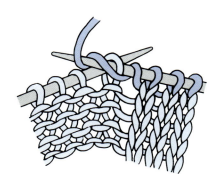

A hole between a purl and a knit stitch
Take the yarn over the needle and then knit the next stitch. This, too, is called 'yarn over needle' (**yon**).

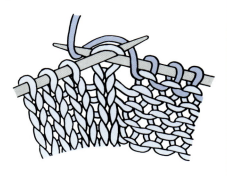

Making a larger hole
It is sometimes necessary to create a larger hole within a lace pattern and this is done by making two extra loops instead of one. This is normally worked between two knit stitches. Bring the yarn forward over the needle, and then all the way around the needle again; knit the next stitch. This is normally referred to as 'yarn forward twice' (**[yf] twice**).

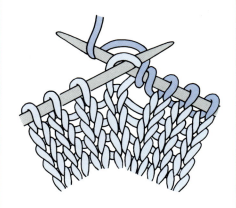

Increasing twice into a stitch

It is sometimes necessary to make three stitches where there was only one stitch before. This often happens where an increase is required in ribbing or where a large number of stitches is increased across a row. It is also used in forming bobbles. There are three common methods of doing this; a pattern will tell you which method to use.

Method 1

Knit into the front of the stitch, bring the yarn forward and purl into the same stitch, then take the yarn back and knit the same stitch again, then slip the original stitch off the left-hand needle. This is called 'work [knit one, purl one, knit one (k1, p1, k1)] into next stitch'.

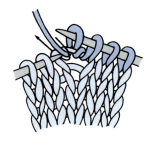

Method 2

This method makes a small hole in the work. Knit into the front of the stitch, bring the yarn forward, then knit into the stitch again, taking the yarn over the top of the right-hand needle. This is called 'work [knit one, yarn forward, knit one (k1, yf, k1)] into the next stitch'.

Method 3

This is normally used in stocking stitch as the stitch is knitted into three times. It produces a relatively small hole in the work. Knit into the front of the stitch, then into the back, then into the front again before slipping the stitch off the left-hand needle. In some publications this is written 'knit front, back, front (kfbf) into next stitch'.

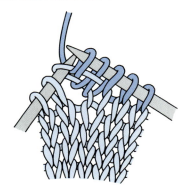

Mitres and corners

It is often necessary to shape a piece of knitting so that it fits around a corner for example, at the front of a V-neck or the corners of a square neck. This is done by increasing (for an outer corner) or decreasing (for an inner corner) at either side of a central stitch.

For an outer corner work to the corner stitch. Increase one stitch using the 'Making a stitch' method (see STARTING STITCHES page 16) or the eyelet method (see pages 6 and 7), knit the next stitch (or purl on a wrong side row), increase one stitch as before, then complete the row.

Depending on the angle of the corner, increase on every row or every alternate row as required. To keep the cast-off

Types of Knitting

edge flat it may be necessary to increase on the cast-off row also.

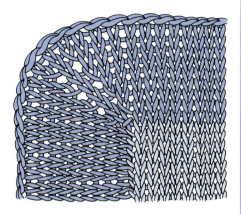

worked on the cast-off row in order to keep it flat.

For an inner corner work to two stitches before the corner stitch, work two stitches together, knit the corner stitch (or purl on the wrong side), work two stitches together in the opposite direction to the first decrease, then complete the row. For example, knit to two stitches before the corner stitch, sl 1, k1, psso (right slope), k1 (corner stitch), k2tog (left slope), knit to end. Working the decreases to slope towards each other ensures that the corner is symmetrical.

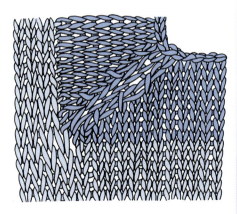

Shaped or mitred V-neckband

This is usually worked in ribbing. The stitches are picked up around the neck (see STARTING STITCHES, page 22) and the shaping is formed by decreasing at either side of the centre-front stitch which should be a knit stitch on the right side of the work. The number of stitches decreased depends upon the angle of the V-neck shaping but the rib pattern must be maintained on every row. The decreasing should also be

FAIR ISLE KNITTING

'Fair Isle' is a general term used for multi-coloured stocking stitch patterns in which two or more colours in a small repeat pattern are used across a single row of knitting. Authentic Fair Isle knitting originated in the Shetland Islands, although similar patterns can be found in traditional Scandinavian garments. The patterns are built up from small basic motifs which are repeated, often in a striped formation, to give complex, colourful designs. Despite the apparent complexity, these patterns rarely contain more than two colours in a single row. The term 'jacquard' is sometimes used instead of 'Fair Isle' but this properly describes colour patterns worked using the intarsia method (see page 10).

TIP

Remember: the key to successful knitting is **tension** or gauge. **Always** check your tension against that given in the pattern and change the needle size if necessary until you obtain the required stitches/rows over the specified measurement.

Types of Knitting

There are two basic methods of working Fair Isle patterns: carrying or 'stranding' the unused yarn across the wrong side of the work, and 'weaving' the two yarns together on the wrong side to avoid leaving long strands of yarn at the back. If you are adding a Fair Isle pattern to a stocking stitch garment, bear in mind that the tension will probably not be the same. Generally the stitches tend to be 'squarer' than in plain stocking stitch; in other words, the number of stitches to 10 cm [4 ins] is often the same as the number of rows to the same measurement, whereas in plain stocking stitch there are more rows than stitches. Always work a tension piece beforehand, as tension can vary enormously between different Fair Isle patterns.

Stranding colours

For this method the colour not in use is carried **loosely** across the wrong side of the work. If strands must be carried over more than six stitches, there is a danger that they could be pulled when the garment is put on or taken off. To avoid this you should twist together the yarn being used with the yarn not in use every third or fourth stitch.

As well as mastering the technique of working with two colours, it is vital to watch out for problems with the tension. The yarn must be stranded very loosely - loosely enough to maintain the elasticity of the fabric; this is difficult to achieve until you have practised the techniques involved and feel relaxed with the work. If you pull the strands even slightly you will buckle the work, giving the finished fabric a puckered, uneven appearance, and thus making the piece too small.

1. On a knit row, hold the first colour in your right hand and the second colour in your left hand (see STARTING STITCHES, page 8). Work as normal with the first colour carrying the second loosely across the wrong side of the work.

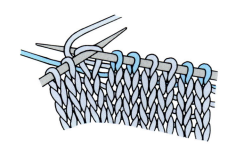

2. When the second colour is required, insert the right-hand needle into the next stitch and draw through a loop of the left-hand yarn; carry the yarn in the right hand loosely across the wrong side until next required.

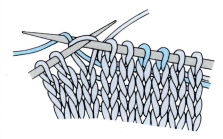

3. On a purl row, work as usual with the first colour held in the right hand, holding the second colour in the left hand.

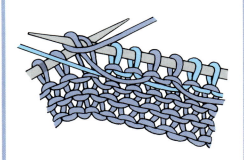

4. To purl a stitch in the second colour, insert the right-hand needle purlwise into the next stitch and draw through a loop of the left-hand yarn.

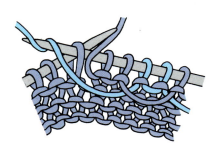

If there are more than six stitches worked in one colour, cross the yarns over each other on every third or fourth stitch to avoid long, loose strands or 'floats'. Simply lay the colour not in use across the yarn being used before working the next stitch.

Stranded knitting should look neat on the wrong side as well as the right. Keeping each colour in the same hand throughout and taking both of them to the end of the rows (twisting them together once at the end of the row to keep them in place) helps to give the fabric a professional appearance.

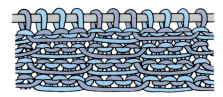

If you find it awkward to hold the yarns in both hands, simply work as usual, dropping the yarn not in use and picking it up again when required, making sure to keep it loose. Always carry the same colour across the top throughout the row for a neat appearance on the wrong side and to prevent the yarns from becoming twisted.

Weaving

Weaving is a method of looping the colour not in use around the yarn being used on every stitch to create a woven effect on the wrong side of the work. The back of a woven fabric looks extremely neat but this method distorts the shape of the stitches and alters the tension. Unless the pattern specifically states that this method should be used, **do not** weave the yarn in but follow the stranding method. Weaving also tends to create a solid, less elastic fabric than the stranding method.

The following diagrams of the right and wrong sides of the work show how the yarns are twisted together to produce the woven effect.

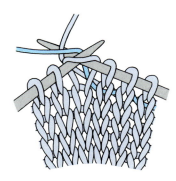

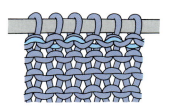

Types of Knitting

Working colour patterns from a chart

Knitting instructions for a Fair Isle pattern are usually given **in chart form**. This gives a visual impression of how the design will look when knitted. A single pattern repeat of the complete design (which must be worked across the width of the fabric) is shown as a chart on a squared grid. The colours in the pattern are represented either by symbols identified in an adjacent key or by colours corresponding to the yarns.

Each square on the chart represents a single stitch; each horizontal line of squares, a row of knitting. The details of how to follow a chart are usually given with the pattern but generally the following rules apply.

Rows

For stocking stitch, work across a line of squares from right to left for the knit rows, then follow the line immediately above, from left to right, for the purl rows. Odd numbers - 1, 3, 5 etc - at the right-hand edge usually indicate the knit rows, while even numbers - 2, 4, 6 etc - at the left-hand edge denote the purl rows. If the pattern is completely symmetrical, every row may be read from right to left. To make following a chart easier, use a row counter or place a ruler above the row being worked and move it up as each row is completed.

Stitches

Usually only one repeat of the pattern is given in the chart and this must be repeated across the width of the fabric. This section is usually contained within bold vertical lines with a bracketed indication that it is to be repeated across the row. There may be extra stitches at either end; these are edge stitches worked at the beginning and end of rows to complete the pattern so that the rows are symmetrical or 'balanced'.

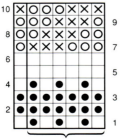

Rep these 6 sts

TIP

Because the edge of a Fair Isle fabric tends to be a little untidy, always take in a whole stitch when joining seams. Although this makes a rather bulky seam it looks neater on the right side.

INTARSIA

'Intarsia' is the name give to colour knitting in which the pattern is worked in large blocks or over large areas at a time, requiring separate balls of yarn to be used for each area of colour. There can be any number of colours across a row. These are not stranded across the back of the work but picked up and dropped where the pattern dictates so that the fabric is the normal thickness. Generally intarsia knitting is worked in stocking stitch (although it can be worked in any textured pattern) and is used for large geometric patterns, individual motifs and pictorial knitting.

Intarsia patterns are usually given in chart form; sometimes a complete section of a garment is shown if the pattern is large and non-repetitive.

This technique (also called motif knitting) can produce beautiful results if worked correctly. Because you will be working with several separate lengths of yarn, there may be a number of ends to be sewn in once the garment is completed. Do not try to cut corners by using the stranding or weaving method as this will alter the tension, producing an unattractive result.

An important feature of this type of knitting is that you must always twist the two yarns when you change colour; otherwise you will leave a hole

Types of Knitting

or, if colours are changed at the same place over several rows, a long slit. Always cross the yarns over on the **wrong side** of the work.

Twisting yarns together

Vertical line
When the colour change is in a vertical line, work to the colour change then, making sure both yarns are at the wrong side of the work, drop the first colour, pick up the second colour and bring it under and around the first colour to cross the yarns over before working the next stitch. On a wrong side row, make sure both yarns are at the front (wrong side) of the work. Drop the first colour, pick up the second colour, and bring it under and around the first colour before working the next stitch. This technique ensures that the yarns are crossed on every row and gives a neat, unbroken vertical line on the right side. Work the first stitch in each colour firmly to prevent a gap forming between the colours.

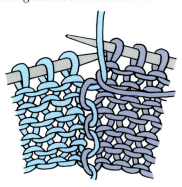

Diagonal slant to the right
When the colour change slants to the right, and a right side row is in progress, the yarns are crossed as shown below. Take the first colour in front of the second colour, drop it, then pick up the second colour and work with it, thus twisting the two colours together. On a wrong side row the yarns will cross automatically because of the direction of the diagonal slant.

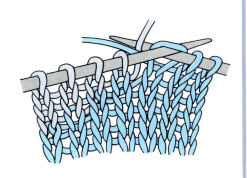

Diagonal slant to the left
When the diagonal slants to the left, and a wrong side row is in progress, the yarns are crossed as shown below. On a right side row the yarns cross automatically.

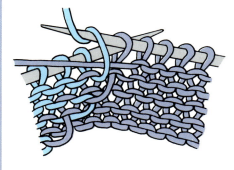

Leave a long end of yarn at the beginning and end of each area of colour - because they lie within the work it is important to secure them carefully. Draw the end up firmly before securing it; otherwise the adjacent stitch will appear loose on the right side. Run the ends through the line of the colour change which will make them relatively invisible.

Using bobbins

Where two or more colours are used in a row, or when the same colour is used in a number of places, it can be difficult to avoid tangling the yarn. Using bobbins keeps the yarns separate by allowing them to hang at the back of the work in the correct position until needed. They are ideal for motif knitting where only a small length of yarn is required.

Bobbins are shaped pieces of plastic with slits in the ends through which the yarn is released as required. They are obtainable at most knitting shops; alternatively you can make your own out of stiff card. Make sure that the bobbin holds the yarn securely, allowing you to unwind a controlled amount of yarn at a time. Use a separate bobbin for each block of colour, winding on sufficient yarn to complete an entire area if possible.

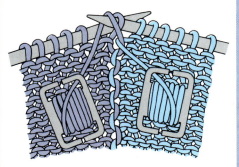

KNITTING IN THE ROUND

The technique of knitting in the round on circular or double-pointed needles produces a seamless fabric. If the knitting is worked without shaping, it produces a tubular shape. By casting on just a few stitches and increasing at regular intervals, it is possible to make a hat shape, or a flat medallion.

Until the end of the 19th century most garments were knitted in the round and today many traditional garments, such as Icelandic sweaters and Guernseys, are still constructed in this way. However, the most common use of circular knitting today is for working neckbands and armbands. These are knitted after the side and shoulder or raglan seams have been joined. Although it is possible to knit these flat and seam the ends together, knitting in the round achieves a neater and more comfortable result. For the same reasons, socks and gloves are normally worked in the round.

Another use for circular knitting is the working of yokes. Normally the front, back and sleeves of the sweater are worked separately on a pair of needles, then a circular needle is used to pick up stitches on all four edges and the yoke is worked in the round, with decreases placed at suitable intervals for shaping. At the neck it is normally necessary to change to a set of double-pointed needles as there are usually too few stitches to reach around even the shortest circular needle. It is also possible to work from the neck downwards and to work the torso and sleeves also in the round.

There are several advantages to working in the round. It is somewhat quicker, since the knitting is never turned at the end of a row. Because the right side of the work is always facing you and every row of a stocking stitch fabric is knitted, the common problem of purl rows being worked more loosely, and thus producing ridges on the right side, does not arise. The number of rows worked for the back and front will always be the same and there are fewer seams to join.

Colour patterns are easier to follow. By looking at the right side all the time you can see how the pattern is developing. The colour not in use is always at the back of the work.

Types of Knitting

for circular knitting. Cast on the stitches for the back and front together and remember to reverse the instructions for the wrong-side rows (that is knit instead of purl and vice versa). Rewrite the stitch pattern instructions as appropriate or, if these are in chart form, substitute the correct symbols on the wrong side rows. The work will have to be divided at the armholes and worked in rows as given in the pattern. For the sleeves, cast on the number of stitches stated and join them into a ring. Work the increases at the underarm edges (that is the beginning and end of each round). Remember when working in rib, that the same stitches are knitted and purled on every round.

> **TIP**
>
> A slip marker is required to mark the beginning of a round in circular knitting or certain parts of a pattern. Plastic ring markers can be used, or you can make one by tying a loop in a short piece of contrasting yarn.

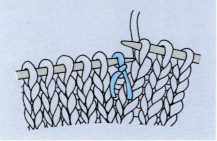

Using a circular needle

A circular needle, or twin pin, has two pointed ends joined by a length of flexible nylon. This kind of needle comes in a range of sizes, from 40 cm [16 ins] to 120 cm [47 ins]. For each size there is a minimum number of stitches required - those which, at a given tension, will fit around the needle without stretching (see the table below). Many more than this minimum will, however, fit on the needle.

> **TIP**
>
> The nylon joining the two points of a circular needle should be straightened before use. Immerse the needle in a bowl of hot water for ten to fifteen minutes, then straighten it out by pulling.

1. To start work, cast on to one point the number of stitches required. It is a good idea to wind an elastic band around the other point to prevent the stitches from slipping off.

2. Spread the stitches along the whole length of the needle and check to make sure that they are not twisted. This step is **vital**; once the work is joined into a circle the stitches cannot be untwisted.

3. Hold the needle so that the point with the first cast-on stitch is in your left hand, with the ball end of the yarn on the right-hand point. Place a marker over the right-hand point and work the first stitch on the left-hand point, pulling the yarn firmly to prevent a gap.

4. Work around to the marker to complete one round. Slip the marker and continue with the next round. Proceed in this manner, always slipping the marker at the beginning of a round and pulling the yarn firmly at this point.

Tension Stitches to		Lengths of circular needle available and minimum number of stitches required						
1 inch	10cm	40cm	50cm	60cm	70cm	80cm	100cm	120cm
5	20	80	99	117	137	157	196	232
5½	22	88	109	129	151	173	216	256
6	24	96	119	141	165	189	236	280
6½	26	104	129	153	179	205	255	303
7	28	112	138	164	192	220	275	327
7½	30	120	148	176	206	236	294	350
8	32	128	158	188	220	252	314	374
8½	34	136	168	200	234	268	334	398
9	36	144	178	212	248	284	353	421

Types of Knitting

Using double-pointed needles

Double-pointed needles must be used if you have only a few stitches. These are most commonly available in sets of four. The stitches are divided evenly on to three of the needles and the remaining needle is used for the knitting. As each needle becomes free, it becomes the working needle.

1. Cast the required number of stitches on to an ordinary needle or circular needle, then slip one-third of them on to each double-pointed needle. (This is easier than casting on to the double-pointed needles).

2. Make sure that the stitches are not twisted, then draw the needles into a triangular shape as shown. Place a marker on the needle holding the last cast-on stitch, then use the free needle to work the first stitch to the left. Pull the yarn across tightly to prevent a gap.

3. When you have finished working all the stitches on one needle, continue with those on the next. At the end of the round slip the marker and begin the next round.

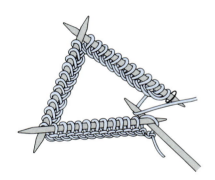

Working into the back of a stitch

Knitwise

Insert the right-hand needle from right to left into the **back** of the next stitch on the left-hand needle, wind the yarn around the point of the right-hand needle, and draw a loop back through the stitch, dropping the original stitch off the left-hand needle. This is abbreviated as **KB1**.

Purlwise

From the back, insert the right-hand needle from left to right into the **back** of the next stitch on the left-hand needle, wind the yarn around the right-hand needle and draw through a loop, dropping the stitch off the left-hand needle. This is abbreviated as **PB1**.

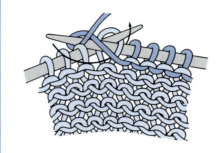

CABLE VARIATIONS

Once you have mastered the use of a cable needle to cross stitches over (see STARTING STITCHES page 19), you will find that there is an enormous variety of effects that can be created in this way. Cables can be used to make diamonds, lattices, figures-of-eight and many other variations. The following techniques are used frequently in Aran knitting to create more intricate panels than the basic rope cables.

In this book the terms 'cross' and 'cable' refer to crossing knit stitches over knit stitches. The term 'twist' is used where knit stitches are crossed over purl stitches (or vice versa).

Twisting stitches

Many cable patterns involve two or more stitches travelling diagonally across a background fabric, either as a lattice pattern or as part of a more intricate cable design. Altering the direction of a column of stitches requires a 'twisting' technique using a cable needle. The most common twists are T3B (twist three back) and T3F (twist three front). Two stitches in stocking stitch are moved across a reverse stocking stitch background by crossing them successively over one purl stitch on alternate rows. The number of stitches in a twist can vary (for example, three stitches in stocking stitch can be moved across two stitches in reverse stocking stitch) but the basic technique remains the same.

Twist three back (T3B)

1. On a right side row, work to one stitch before the two in stocking stitch. Slip the next stitch on to a cable needle and leave it at the back of the work.

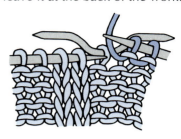

2. Knit the next two stitches on the left-hand needle.

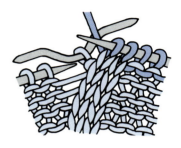

3. Now purl the stitch on the cable needle. This produces a twist to the **right**.

Twist three front (T3F)

1. On a right-side row, work to the two stocking stitch stitches. Slip these on to a cable needle and leave them at the front of the work.

2. Purl the next stitch on the left-hand needle.

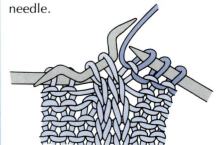

Garment Styles and Features

3. Knit the two stitches on the cable needle. This produces a twist to the **left**.

The actual name of any cable may vary from one publication to another but working details are always given either in the abbreviations or where the technique first occurs in the instructions.

BANDS AND BORDERS

Most stocking stitch-based knitted fabrics tend to curl at the edges and so must be finished with a band or border. A double-sided fabric, such as garter stitch or one of the moss stitch variations, will lie flat and may not need any neatening unless the style of the garment calls for an edging. Some borders, such as ribbed welts and cuffs, are normally knitted in with the garment; others, such as neckbands and collars are typically worked on stitches picked up along a shaped edge; alternatively they are sewn on. Whichever method is used, the relationship between the tension/gauge of the main part of the garment and the edging requires consideration.

A ribbed welt or cuff is usually designed so that its fabric fits more snugly than the material of the main part of the garment. However, the difference in row tension between ribbing and stocking stitch means that ribbed front edges cannot be knitted at the same time as the main part of the garment. There are fewer rows to the centimetre or inch in ribbing than in stocking stitch knitted on the same size needles. If the two were knitted together, the front edge would lie longer than the main part of the cardigan, giving a wavy or distorted edge. For this reason the stitches for a vertically knitted front band in rib are usually left on a holder at the top of the ribbed welt and knitted up afterwards on the smaller needles used for the welt.

Neck and arm bands

Armholes of sleeveless garments and most necklines need to be finished with a border. This can be worked backwards or forwards on two needles before all the seams are joined, or on a circular needle or set of double-pointed needles after the adjacent seams are joined.

First pick up and knit the required number of stitches around the edge (see STARTING STITCHES page 22). Work in the appropriate stitch (usually rib for its elasticity) until the border is the required depth. The border can then be cast off **loosely**; or, if it is to be doubled, the stitches can be slipped on to a length of yarn and sewn in place (see page 18).

Cardigan front bands

Front bands or borders can either be knitted up with the garment, picked up and knitted along the edge or knitted up separately and sewn in place.

Bands knitted in with the garment tend to be either in garter stitch or moss stitch, as ribbed bands would be too loose if worked on the same size needles as the main body. A few stitches at the front edge will be worked in garter stitch or moss stitch, and the buttonholes worked in the centre of these stitches. For a **round-neck cardigan** the border stitches are cast off or slipped on to a safety pin at the start of the neck shaping. For a **V-neck cardigan** the neck decreases are worked at the edge of the main fabric **outside** the border stitches. At the top edge, the border stitches are left on a safety pin and the shoulder stitches cast off; then the border is continued until it fits across to the centre-back neck. The two ends can either be cast off and joined in a seam or grafted or cast off together.

Bands worked on picked-up stitches are generally worked in rib for a firm edge. The stitches should be picked up through a whole stitch at the edge of the main section; make sure that the first and last stitches at the top and bottom of the piece are worked into. For a **round-neck cardigan** the stitches would be picked up after the neckband is worked so that the front bands form an unbroken line. For a **V-neck cardigan** the band is worked on stitches picked up along the entire front and neck edges combined. Make sure that the same number of stitches is picked up from the lower edge to the start of the neck shaping on each front to ensure that buttons and buttonholes correspond.

Vertical sewn-on front bands can be worked separately and sewn on

Garment Styles and Features

afterwards. If the band is in the same stitch pattern as the welt, however, the usual practice is to include the band stitches in the welt and then slip them on to a safety pin when beginning the main fabric. When the band is knitted up an extra stitch should be cast on at the inside edge; this will be taken into the seam.

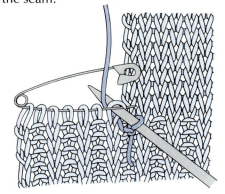

To ensure that the band lies flat, it should be **slightly stretched** and pinned in position as you are working. Remember when measuring that the front edge of a stocking stitch cardigan is likely to be a bit stretched anyway, so measure with the main piece lying flat. The centre of the work is the length to go by.

For a **round-neck cardigan** the front bands are knitted up until they reach the start of the front neck shaping, and the stitches are then cast off or held on a safety pin to be worked with the neckband.

For a **V-neck cardigan** the front bands are knitted up until they reach up the entire length of the front edge and across to the centre of the back neck. The stitches are then cast off and sewn together or slipped on to a safety pin to be cast off or grafted together.

Sewing on front bands

As the front bands are a strong focal point of a cardigan, take care when sewing them on to give the work a professional finish.

First lay the back flat on a table and position the fronts on top, matching shoulders and cast-on edges. Check that any horizontal patterns are level across the garment and pin the band in place, stretching it evenly. On most stocking stitch garments the band can be sewn to the main garment row for row using a mattress stitch seam (see page 17) for an extremely neat finish. If the band cannot be joined row for row, adjust the stitching as necessary, depending on which section has more rows. If this type of seam is not appropriate, use a flat seam (see STARTING STITCHES page 23) - never backstitch. Do not ease a band in to fit the front edge if it is too long - this will give a fluted edge. Unravel the extra rows from the top edge and re-pin the band in place. It is always advisable to sew the button band in place and mark button positions **before** knitting the buttonhole band. In this way you can ensure that the correct number of rows are knitted between buttonholes.

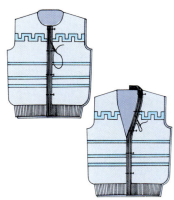

BUTTONS AND BUTTONHOLES

A buttonhole may seem an insignificant detail but a garment can be ruined by badly worked buttonholes or the wrong buttons. Choose the buttons after you have knitted the button band and sewn it in place. That way you have a much clearer idea of the size and quantity of buttons you could use. You need not follow the pattern's specifications; you might prefer to use more but smaller buttons, or fewer larger ones.

The methods of producing buttonholes described here and on the next page are shown worked in ribbed bands but they can also be worked in garter stitch or moss stitch bands, and are sometimes worked within the main fabric. Worked correctly, they all provide a neat finish which should not require further stitching.

TIP

Before working a buttonhole in the front band, knit a small sample of the band including one or more sample buttonholes. You may find that you need to amend the number of cast-off stitches to suit your choice of button - or simply to practise your buttonhole technique.

Eyelet/round buttonhole

This is the simplest way of making a small, neat buttonhole, suitable for a small button; it is often used for baby clothes.

1. Work to the position of the buttonhole (usually the centre stitch of the band).

2. Wind the yarn around the needle to make an extra stitch (see page 6), then work the next two stitches together. You will still have the same number of loops on the needle as before, as the extra loop replaces the one decreased stitch.

3. Work to the end of the row. On the following row work into all stitches including the loop.

In a ribbed band the buttonhole looks neater if it replaces a purl stitch rather than a knit stitch so that the vertical lines of the rib are not broken. In this case you would work on a right-side row to the purl stitch to be replaced, then work 'yarn forward, knit two together'.

Horizontal/cast-off buttonhole

This buttonhole is worked over two rows. A given number of stitches is cast off in the first row and then the same number is cast on in the following row. The number of stitches depends on the size of the button and the thickness of the yarn - a thick yarn making the hole somewhat smaller.

1. On a right-side row work to the position for the buttonhole, cast off the required number of stitches, then work to the end of the row.

2. On the next row work to the cast-off stitches, turn and cast on the same number of stitches using the cable method (see STARTING STITCHES page 10). **Note:** before placing the last new stitch on the left-hand needle,

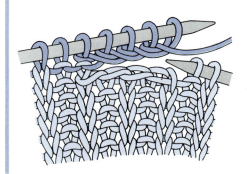

Garment Styles and Features

bring the yarn to the front of the work between the needle points.

3. Turn the work again and complete the row. Bringing the yarn between the last two cast-on stitches ensures that there is no gap at the end of the buttonhole.

One-row buttonhole

This variation of the horizontal buttonhole is neat and self-reinforcing which makes it very strong, although less elastic than other buttonholes.

1. On a right-side row work to the position of the buttonhole. Bring the yarn to the front (unless it is already there) and slip the next stitch, then take the yarn to the back and leave it there.

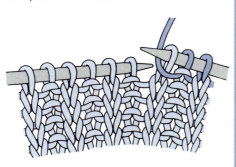

2. Slip the next stitch, then cast off the first slipped stitch.

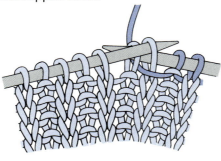

3. Repeat this step to cast off the required number of stitches for the buttonhole. Return the last slipped stitch to the left-hand needle.

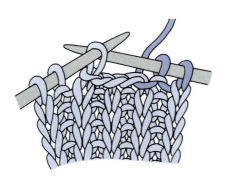

4. Turn the work and take the yarn to the back. Using the cable method, cast on all the buttonhole stitches plus one extra stitch.

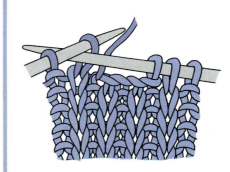

5. Before placing this last stitch on the left-hand needle bring the yarn forward. Turn the work. Slip the last stitch on the right-hand needle back on to the left-hand needle and work it together with the next stitch. Work to the end of the row.

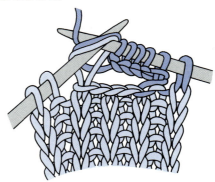

Vertical buttonhole

A vertical buttonhole is quite easy to work and depending on the thickness of the yarn, a few rows will make quite a deep opening.

1. First mark the button positions on the button band, then decide how long you want the buttonhole to be. Mark this length equally balanced above and below the button.

2. On the buttonhole band work to the position of the buttonhole, then divide the work by dropping the old yarn, joining in another ball of yarn and working to the end of the row.

3. For the next few rows - those required for the buttonhole - continue to work each side separately so that the band is divided into two parts.

4. To close the buttonhole, work across the whole row with the original end of yarn. To strengthen the top and bottom of the buttonhole, thread each spare end of yarn into a tapestry

Making up

needle and work a couple of stitches through the wrong side of the work.

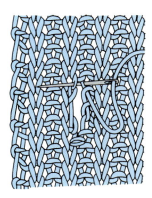

Sewing on buttons

Buttons are available in many shapes, colours and sizes and can add a fashionable touch to an otherwise plain garment. They usually have two or four holes all the way through the button or a shank at the back.

For a heavy cardigan or jacket it is advisable to choose a shank button, as the shank allows room for the button-hole band.

As buttons are an important feature of a garment, it is important that they be sewn on correctly.

Place the two fronts together so that the bands overlap with the buttonhole band on top and so that any horizontal patterns are exactly level across the garment. Thread a tapestry needle with contrasting thread and insert the needle through the buttonhole and into the button band. Make a small stitch to mark the position of the button.

Sew the button in place using the knitting yarn or a finer matching yarn or thread if the original yarn is too thick to pass through the hole. First, make a small backstitch to secure the yarn, then sew the button to the band using four or five stitches. Do not pull the yarn tightly or it will pull the band out of shape. Fasten the yarn off securely on the wrong side.

It maybe advisable on a heavy garment to sew a small lightweight button or piece of fabric on the inside of the band to take some of the strain.

MAKING UP - PROFESSIONAL TECHNIQUES

Mattress stitch seam

This seam is also know as a **ladder stitch seam, running stitch seam** or **invisible seam.** It is the seam that the professionals use wherever possible, and if you practise working it you will find that it is an easy method for obtaining a perfect finish. Even if you have always used a backstitch or oversewn seam, try this method and you will be surprised how easy it is and how much better the seams look and feel.

Ideally, the edges to be joined should have the same number of rows. When knitting the garment, use a row counter to ensure this; minor discrepancies can be compensated for but this is to be avoided if possible.

Mattress stitch should be worked either one whole stitch or half a stitch in from the edge depending on the neatness of the edge and the thickness of the fabric. It can even be worked on shaped edges, because as you are working from the right side, it easy to see where you are and to keep the seam neat.

When starting off, do not fasten the thread but leave a long end which can be secured by running it back along the edge when the seam is completed. If the seam needs to be undone, simply pull this end, thus drawing the yarn through the stitches.

Selvedge Stitches

If the fabric you are knitting has a repeat - that is, a texture or colour pattern - it is advisable to add an extra stitch to each edge. This edge or selvedge stitch is taken into the seam, leaving the pattern stitches intact, so that the repeat runs across the seam wihout interruption. Garment patterns often provide for a selvedge; if the one you are working does not, you can add a selvedge stitch to each edge. Knit these stitches on right side rows and purl on wrong side rows.

Another kind of selvedge can be worked on stocking stitch to make the edges firmer than they normally are on this fabric. Simply knit the first stitch knitwise on a right side row, then knit to the end. Slip the first stitch purlwise on a wrong side row and purl to the end.

Joining stocking stitch or a stocking stitch-based fabric

1. Place the two pieces, right side up, on a flat surface with their edges together. Thread a tapestry needle with yarn and insert the needle at the lower left-hand corner between the edge stitch and the second stitch as shown. Pass the needle under the first row, then bring it back through to the front.

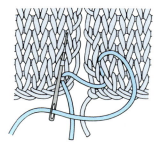

2. Take it to the opposite side and work under the first two rows.

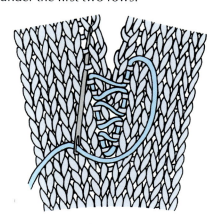

3. Return to the left side and work under the next two rows. Continue in the zigzag pattern, always taking the needle under the strands that correspond exactly to those on the other side and going into the hole that the last stitch on that side came out of, taking care not to miss any rows.

The secret of good mattress stitching is to keep the seam elastic without allowing it to stretch too much. The best way to do this is to work loosely for approximately 5 cm [2 ins], then pull the thread very firmly so that the stitches are held together quite tightly. Now stretch the seam slightly to give the required amount of elasticity, then continue with the next section of the seam.

The finished seam is almost impossible to detect on the right side and leaves only a small neat ridge on the wrong side. If only half a stitch is taken in (working through the centre of the

Making Up

edge stitch rather than between this stitch and the next), the ridge on the wrong side will be even finer. This method is recommended for thicker yarns, provided that the edge stitch has been worked firmly and neatly.

Note: If you work a slipped stitch at the beginning of every row (as recommended in some printed patterns) you should always work mattress stitch one whole stitch in from the edge.

Joining reverse stocking stitch fabric or background

If the purl side of the fabric is the right side, you may find that you achieve a better effect by working under one row at a time rather than the two rows as described for stocking stitch.

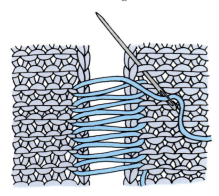

Joining single rib

When joining two single-rib sections, it is best to take in only half a stitch on either side so that when the two pieces are drawn together one complete knit stitch is formed along the seam. Note that the ribbing must contain an uneven number of stitches so that all edges consist of knit stitches. Wider rib patterns may need to be adjusted to make a symmetrical join possible.

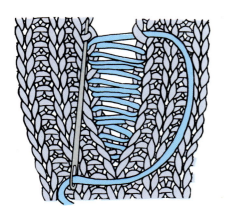

Joining two cast-off edges

Two cast-off edges can be joined using mattress stitch provided that they are straight (that is, unshaped) and have the same number of stitches.

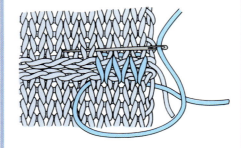

Joining two sections of different tensions

When joining two pieces where the number of rows may be different - for example, joining a ribbed front band to a stocking stitch or patterned front - work as follows: lay the two pieces side by side then, using safety pins, pin the sections together at the lower and top edges, stretching the ribbing slightly (unless otherwise instructed) and taking in the edge stitch of each piece. Pin again halfway between the two pins, then halve this distance again. Continue in this way until there are enough pins to keep the edges together, then join the two edges working under one or two rows as necessary, removing the pins as you go along.

Use this method also when joining a cast-off edge (such as the top of a drop shoulder sleeve) to a side edge. Make sure that both edges lie flat and work under one or two rows or stitches as necessary, making sure the seam retains its elasticity. In the case of a shaped, set-in sleeve, it is better to start at the centre and work downwards along either side.

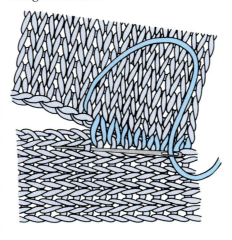

Sewing a neckband in place

In finishing a double neckband, it is possibly simpler to cast off the stitches (loosely) and then sew the cast-off edge in place on the wrong side. However, it is much neater - and makes a more elastic neckline - to use one of the following methods.

Neckband turned to inside

Do not cast the stitches off but leave them on a length of yarn. Fold the finished neckband in half to the inside and slipstitch the edge loosely to the first row of the neckband, matching stitch for stitch and taking care to catch every one. It is important not to twist the band when stitching or it will appear misshapen. Before fastening off, stretch the neckband so that it will fit comfortably over the head, allowing the yarn to run through the caught stitches, then fasten off securely.

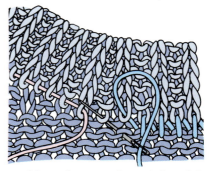

Neckband turned to right side

Another method of finishing a double neckband is to fold the band in half to the outside and backstitch the stitches in place on the right side to form a visible ridge. Finish the neckband with a knit row on the wrong side (this will be the right side when the neckband is turned over), then slip the stitches off the needle and on to two lengths of yarn. Fold the neckband in half to the outside and use one of the strands of yarn to backstitch every stitch to the neck edge, working through the stitches of the last knit row and removing the spare yarn as the stitches are sewn in place.

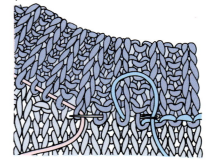

Abbreviations and Symbols

HOW TO READ STITCH CHARTS

Charts are read exactly as the knitting is worked from the bottom to the top. After the last row at the top has been worked, repeat the sequence from row 1. Each symbol represents an instruction. Symbols have been designed to resemble the actual appearance of the knitting.

Before starting to knit, look up all the symbols on your chosen chart so that you are familiar with the techniques involved. **Make sure you understand the difference between working similar symbols on a right side row and a wrong side row.**

Each square represents a stitch and each horizontal line a row. Place a ruler above the line you are working. If you are new to chart reading try comparing the charted instructions with the written ones.

Coloured patterns include suggested colours indicated by a letter at the beginning of each row.

Right Side and Wrong Side Rows

A 'right side row' is one in which the right side is facing you as you work and a 'wrong side row' is one in which the wrong side is facing as you work. Row numbers are shown at the side of the charts **at the beginning of the row.** Right side rows are always read from right to left. Wrong side rows are always read from left to right.

Symbols on the charts are shown as they appear from the right side of the work. Therefore, a horizontal dash stands for a purl 'bump' on the right side regardless of whether it was achieved by purling on a right side row or knitting on a wrong side row. To make things clearer, symbols on right side rows are slightly darker than on wrong side rows.

Pattern Repeats and Multiples

In charted instructions the pattern repeat is contained between heavier vertical lines. The extra stitches not included in the pattern repeat are there to 'balance' the row or make it symmetrical and are worked only once.

Panels

Panels are patterns worked over a given number of stitches without necessarily being repeated.

All the panels in this book have been worked on a suggested background stitch. On the charts this is indicated by two stitches at either side of the panel. To work any of the panels you must cast on enough stitches to work the panel plus the required number of background stitches on each side.

Abbreviations and Symbols

The following abbreviations and symbols include all those used in this book.

Alt = alternate; **beg** = beginning; **cm** = centimetre(s); **dec** = decrease; **inc** = increase; **ins** = inches; **k** = knit; **KB1** = knit into back of stitch; **m** = metre(s); **mm** = millimetre(s); **p** = purl; **PB1** = purl into back of stitch; **psso** = pass slipped stitch over; **p2sso** = pass 2 slipped stitches over; **p3sso** = pass 3 slipped stitches over; **rep** = repeat; **sl** = slip; **st(s)** = stitch(es); **st st** = stocking stitch (1 row knit, 1 row purl); **tog** = together; **tbl** through back of loops; **yb** = yarn back; **yf** = yarn forward; **yfrn** = yarn forward and round needle; **yon** = yarn over needle; **yrn** = yarn round needle.

Inc 1 (Inc 1K or Inc 1P) = Increase 1 st knitwise or purlwise by knitting or purling into front and back of next st.

M1 (M1K or M1P) = Make 1 st knitwise or purlwise by picking up strand of yarn lying between last st worked and next st and knitting or purling into back of it.

Note: Symbols are dark on right side rows and light on wrong side rows.

I	K knit on right side rows
−	K knit on wrong side rows
−	P purl on right side rows
I	P purl on wrong side rows
V	KB1 knit into back of st on right side rows
<	KB1 knit into back of st on wrong side rows
<	PB1 purl into back of st on right side rows
V	PB1 purl into back of st on wrong side rows
⟋	k2tog on right side rows
⟍	k2tog on wrong side rows
⟍	p2tog on right side rows
⟋	p2tog on wrong side rows

Sample Chart

- 1 stitch
- 1 row
- wrong side rows start this side
- right side rows start this side
- Rep these 12 sts — pattern repeat
- stitches to balance pattern
- tint indicates instruction involving more than 1 stitch

Note: For meaning of each symbol refer to abbreviations.

Abbreviations and Symbols

k2togtbl on right side rows

k2togtbl on wrong side rows

p2togtbl on right side rows

p2togtbl on wrong side rows

sl1, k1, psso on right side rows

sl 2tog knitwise, k1, p2sso on right side rows

sl 1, k2tog, psso on right side rows

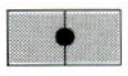

yf, yfrn, yon, yrn (to make a st) on right side rows

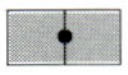

yf, yfrn, yon, yrn (to make a st) on wrong side rows

k3tog on right side rows

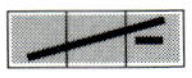

p3tog on right side rows

p3tog on wrong side rows

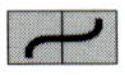

C2B (Cross 2 Back) = slip next st on to cable needle and hold at back of work, knit next st from left-hand needle, then knit st from cable needle.

C2F (Cross 2 Front) = slip next st on to cable needle and hold at front of work, knit next st from left-hand needle, then knit st from cable needle.

T2B (Twist 2 Back) = slip next st on to cable needle and hold at back of work, knit next st from left-hand needle, then purl st from cable needle.

T2F (Twist 2 Front) = slip next st on to cable needle and hold at front of work, purl next st from left-hand needle, then knit st from cable needle.

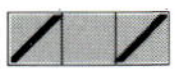

C3B (Cable 3 Back) = slip next st on to cable needle and hold at back of work, knit next 2 sts from left-hand needle, then knit st from cable needle.

C3F (Cable 3 Front) = slip next 2 sts on to cable needle and hold at front of work, knit next st from left-hand needle, then knit sts from cable needle.

T3B (Twist 3 Back) = slip next st on to cable needle and hold at back of work, knit next 2 sts from left-hand needle, then purl st from cable needle.

T3F (Twist 3 Front) = slip next 2 sts on to cable needle and hold at front of work, purl next st from left-hand needle, then knit sts from cable needle.

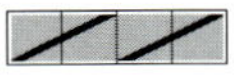

C4B (Cable 4 Back) = slip next 2 sts on to cable needle and hold at back of work, knit next 2 sts from left-hand needle, then knit sts from cable needle.

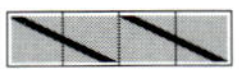

C4F (Cable 4 Front) = slip next 2 sts on to cable needle and hold at front of work, knit next 2 sts from left-hand needle, then knit sts from cable needle.

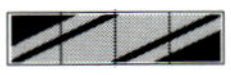

T4B (Twist 4 Back) = slip next 2 sts on to cable needle and hold at back of work, knit next 2 sts from left-hand needle, then purl sts from cable needle.

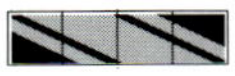

T4F (Twist 4 Front) = slip next 2 sts on to cable needle and hold at front of work, purl next 2 sts from left-hand needle, then knit sts from cable needle.

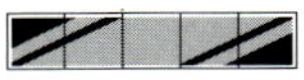

T5R (Twist 5 Right) = slip next 2 sts on to cable needle and hold at back of work, knit next 3 sts from left-hand needle, then purl sts from cable needle.

T5L (Twist 5 Left) = slip next 3 sts on to cable needle and hold at front of work, purl next 2 sts from left-hand needle, then knit sts from cable needle.

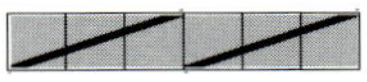

C6B (Cable 6 Back) = slip next 3 sts on to cable needle and hold at back of work, knit next 3 sts from left-hand needle, then knit sts from cable needle.

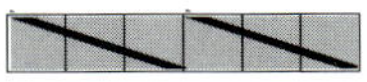

C6F (Cable 6 Front) = slip next 3 sts on to cable needle and hold at front of work, knit next 3 sts from left-hand needle, then knit sts from cable needle.

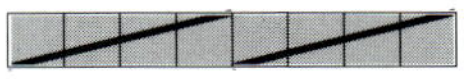

C8B (Cable 8 Back) = slip next 4 sts on to cable needle and hold at back of work, knit next 4 sts from left-hand needle, then knit sts from cable needle.

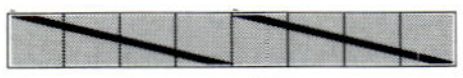

C8F (Cable 8 Front) = slip next 4 sts on to cable needle and hold at front of work, knit next 4 sts from left-hand needle, then knit sts from cable needle.

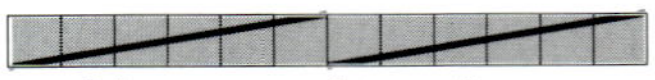

C12B (Cable 12 Back) = slip next 6 sts on to cable needle and hold at back of work, knit next 6 sts from left-hand needle, then knit sts from cable needle.

C12F (Cable 12 Front) = slip next 6 sts on to cable needle and hold at front of work, knit next 6 sts from left-hand needle, then knit sts from cable needle.

Working from Patterns

Instructions are given for the smallest size, larger sizes in round brackets. Figures or instructions in square brackets [ ] should be repeated as stated after the brackets. Where only one figure is given this applies to all sizes.

For American Readers

English terms are used in this book. Note the equivalent American terms:

Tension - Gauge
Cast Off - Bind Off
Stocking Stitch - Stockinette Stitch
Yf, Yfrn, Yon and **Yrn** (to make a st)- Yarn Over

Stitch Pattern Multiples

The multiple or repeat of each stitch pattern plus the number of stitches needed to 'balance' the row is given with the written instructions.

To make working from the written instructions easier, in some instances one extra repeat has been added to the balancing stitches; THESE EXTRA STITCHES ARE NOT NEEDED ON THE CHARTS.

See Little Arrowhead on page 22.
Multiple of 6 sts + 7.
The chart shows the 6 repeat stitches and 1 balancing stitch (7 sts). The written instructions include one extra repeat (multiple of 6 sts + 6 + 1 balancing stitch) therefore a minimum of 11 stitches must be worked.

KNITTING stylish STITCHES

In the following pages you'll find a tempting collection of stitches including lace panels and cables, as well as Fair Isle and intarsia motifs. Also six stylish garments for displaying your knitting expertise.

Woman's Waistcoat

Measurements

To fit bust size	80/85	90/95	100/105	cm
	32/34	36/38	40/42	ins
Finished measurement at bust	105	115	125	cm
	42	46	50	ins
Length to shoulder	70	71	72	cm
	27½	28	28¼	ins

Shown in 90/95 cm [36/38 inch] size

Materials

4 ply knitting yarn	375	400	425	grams
	14	15	16	ounces

Pair needles each size 3¼mm (UK 10, USA 3 or 4) and 2¾ mm (UK 12, USA 2). 2¾mm (UK 12, USA 2) circular needle. Cable needle. 4 buttons.

The quantities of yarn stated are based on average requirements and are therefore approximate.
For abbreviations see pages 19 and 20.

Tension

28 sts and 36 rows = 10 cm [4 ins] square measured over st st using larger needles.

Special Abbreviations

M1 (Make 1 st) = pick up strand of yarn lying between last st worked and next stitch and work into back of it.

C4B (Cable 4 Back) = slip next 2 sts on to cable needle and hold at back of work, knit next 2 sts from left-hand needle, then knit sts from cable needle.

C4F (Cable 4 Front) = slip next 2 sts on to cable needle and hold at front of work, knit next 2 sts from left-hand needle, then knit sts from cable needle.

Back

Using larger needles cast on 171(185-199) sts and commence pattern.

1st row (right side): K31(37-42), *p2, k4, p2, k12, p2, k4, p2*, k53(55-59); rep from * to *, k31(37-42).

2nd row: P31(37-42), *k2, p4, k2, p12, k2, p4, k2*, p53(55-59); rep from * to *, p31(37-42).

3rd row: K2, [k2tog, yf] 14(17-19) times, k1(1-2), *p2, C4F, p2, k1, [k2tog, yf] 5 times, k1, p2, C4B, p2*, k1, [k2tog, yf] 25(26-28) times, k2; rep from * to *, k0(0-1), [k2tog, yf] 14(17-19) times, k3.

4th row: As 2nd row.

5th row: K2, k2tog, yf, k27(33-38), *p2, k4, p2, k2, [k2tog, yf] 4 times, k2, p2, k4, p2*, k53(55-59); rep from * to *, k27(33-38), yf, sl 1, k1, psso, k2.

6th row: P31(37-42), *k2, p4, k2, p12, k2, p4, k2*, p53(55-59); rep from * to *, p31(37-42).

7th row: K2, k2tog, yf, k27(33-38), *p2, C4F, p2, k1, [k2tog, yf] 5 times, k1, p2, C4B, p2*, k53(55-59); rep from * to *, k27(33-38), yf, sl 1, k1, psso, k2.

8th row: As 2nd row.

Rep 5th to 8th rows until back measures 16 cm [6¼ ins] ending with a wrong side row.

Next row: Cast on 6 sts, knit these sts, work in pattern to end.

Next row: Cast on 6 sts, purl these sts, work in pattern to end. 183(197-211) sts.

Next row: K2, [k2tog, yf] 4 times, work in pattern to last 10 sts, [yf, sl 1, k1, psso] 4 times, k2.

Next row: P37(43-48), *k2, p4, k2, p12, k2, p4, k2*, p53(55-59); rep from * to *, p37(43-48).

Next row: K37(43-48), work in pattern to last 37(43-48) sts, knit to end.

Working sts at each side and between panels in st st, work 5 more rows thus ending with a wrong side row.

Shape Sides

Next row: K1, sl 1, k1, psso, work in pattern to last 3 sts, k2tog, k1. Continue to dec 1 st in this way at each end of every following 8th row until 161(175-189) sts remain. Work straight until back measures 45 cm [17¾ ins] ending with a wrong side row.

Shape Armholes

Keeping pattern correct, cast off 8(10-11) sts at beg of next 2 rows. Dec 1 st at each end of next 7(11-13) rows, then every following alt row until 115(117-123) sts remain. Work straight until armholes measure 23(24-25) cm [9(9½-10) ins] measured straight from start of armhole shaping ending with a wrong side row.

Shape Shoulders

Cast off 9 sts at beg of next 6 rows, then 8(8-9) sts at beg of following 2 rows. Cast off remaining 45(47-51) sts.

Left Front

Using larger needles cast on 81(88-95) sts and commence pattern.

1st row (right side): K31(37-42), p2, k4, p2, k12, p2, k4, p2, k22(23-25).

2nd row: P22(23-25), k2, p4, k2, p12, k2, p4, k2, p31(37-42).

3rd row: K2, [k2tog, yf] 14(17-19) times, k1(1-2), p2, C4F, p2, k1, [k2tog, yf] 5 times, k1, p2, C4B, p2, k1(2-2), [k2tog, yf] 9(9-10) times, k3.

4th row: As 2nd row.

5th row: K2, k2tog, yf, k27(33-38), p2, k4, p2, k2, [k2tog, yf] 4 times, k2, p2, k4, p2, k18(19-21), yf, sl 1, k1, psso, k2.

6th row: P22(23-25), k2, p4, k2, p12, k2, p4, k2, p31(37-42).

7th row: K2, k2tog, yf, k27(33-38), p2, C4F, p2, k1, [k2tog, yf] 5 times, k1, p2, C4B, p2, k18(19-21), yf, sl 1, k1, psso, k2.

8th row: As 2nd row.

Rep 5th to 8th rows until front measures 16 cm [6¼ ins] ending with a wrong side row.

Next row: Cast on 6 sts, knit these sts, work in pattern to end. 87(94-101) sts.

Woman's Waistcoat

Work 1 row straight.

Next row: K2, [k2tog, yf] 4 times, work in pattern to end.

Next row: P22(23-25), k2, p4, k2, p12, k2, p4, k2, p37(43-48).

Next row: K37(43-48), work in pattern to end.

Working side edge in st st as on Back, work 5 rows straight, thus ending with a wrong side row.

Shape Side

Next row: K1, sl 1, k1, psso, work in pattern to end.

Dec 1 st at side edge in this way on every following 8th row until 76(83-90) sts remain. Work straight until front measures same as back to start of armhole shaping ending with a wrong side row.

Shape Armhole and Front Slope

1st row: Cast off 8(10-11) sts, work in pattern to last 6 sts, k2tog (neck dec), yf, sl 1, k1, psso, k2.

2nd row: P5, work in pattern to end.

3rd row: K2togtbl, work in pattern to last 5 sts, k1, yf, sl 1, psso, k2.

4th row: P5, work in pattern to last 2 sts, p2togtbl.

★ Dec 1 st at armhole edge on next 5(9-11) rows, then on following 8(8-9) alt rows, **at the same time** dec 1 st at neck edge as before on next and every following 4th row until 46(46-48) sts remain. Keeping armhole edge straight, continue to dec 1 st at neck edge only on every following 4th row until 37 sts remain then every following 6th row until 35(35-36) sts remain. Work straight until front measures same as back to start of shoulder shaping ending at side edge.

Shape Shoulder

Cast off 9 sts at beg of next and following 2 alt rows. Work 1 row. Cast off remaining 8(8-9) sts.

Right Front

Using larger needles cast on 81(88-95) sts and commence pattern.

1st row (right side): K22(23-25), p2, k4, p2, k12, p2, k4, p2, k31(37-42).

2nd row: P31(37-42), k2, p4, k2, p12, k2, p4, k2, p22(23-25).

3rd row: K2, [k2tog, yf] 9(9-10) times, k2(3-3), p2, C4F, p2, k1, [k2tog, yf] 5 times, k1, p2, C4B, p2, k0(0-1), [k2tog, yf] 14(17-19) times, k3.

4th row: As 2nd row.

5th row: K2, k2tog, yf, k18(19-21), p2, k4, p2, k2, [k2tog, yf] 4 times, k2, p2, k4, p2, k27(33-38), yf, sl 1, k1, psso, k2.

6th row: P31(37-42), k2, p4, k2, p12, k2, p4, k2, p22(23-25).

7th row: K2, k2tog, yf, k18(19-21), p2, C4F, p2, k1, [k2tog, yf] 5 times, k1, p2, C4B, p2, k27(33-38), yf, sl 1, k1, psso, k2.

8th row: As 2nd row.

Rep 5th to 8th rows until front measures 16 cm [6¼ ins] ending with a right side row.

Next row: Cast on 6 sts, purl these sts, work in pattern to end. 87(94-101) sts.

Next row: Work in pattern to last 10 sts, [yf, sl 1, k1, psso] 4 times, k2.

Next row: P37(43-48), work in pattern to end.

Working side edge in st st as on Back, work 6 rows straight thus ending with a wrong side row.

Shape Side

Next row: Work in pattern to last 3 sts, k2tog, k1.

Dec 1 st at side edge in this way on every following 8th row until 76(83-90) sts remain. Work straight until front measures same as back to start of armhole shaping ending with a wrong side row.

Shape Armhole and Front Slope

1st row: K2, k2tog, yf, sl 1, k1, psso (neck dec), work in pattern to end.

2nd row: Cast off 8(10-11) sts, work in pattern to last 5 sts, p5.

Complete as given for Left Front from ★ to end.

Finishing and Bands

Block, but do not press.

Lower Back and Vent Edging

Using circular needle and with right side facing, pick up and knit 54 sts down side edge of back from cast on sts to lower edge, 169(183-197) sts along cast on edge and 54 sts up side edge to cast on sts. 277(291-305) sts.

Turning at end of each row continue as follows:

1st row: [P1, k1] 27 times, p1 (mark this st with a contrasting thread), k1, [p1, k1] 2(1-1) times, *work [p1, k1, p1] into next st, [k1, p1] twice, k1; rep from * 25(28-30) times more, work [p1, k1, p1] into next st, k1, [p1, k1] 2(1-2) times, p1 (mark this st with a contrasting thread), [k1, p1] 27 times. 331(351-369) sts.

2nd row: Rib to marked st, M1, k1, M1, rib to next marked st, M1, k1, M1, rib to end.

3rd row: Rib to marked st, p1, rib to next marked st, p1, rib to end.

Rep the last 2 rows twice more, then 2nd row again. 347(367-385) sts. Cast off in rib.

Lower Left Front and Vent Edging

Using circular needle and with right side facing, pick up and knit 79(87-93) sts along cast on edge of left front, then 54 sts up side edge to cast on sts. 133(141-147) sts.

Turning at end of each row continue as follows:

1st row: [P1, k1] 27 times, p1 (mark this st with a contrasting thread), k1, [p1, k1] 2(3-3) times, *work [p1, k1, p1] into next st, [k1, p1] twice, k1; rep from * 10(11-12) times more, work [p1, k1, p1] into next st, k1, [p1, k1] 3 times. 157(167-175) sts.

2nd row: Rib to marked st, M1, k1, M1, rib to end.

3rd row: Rib to marked st, p1, rib to end.

Rep the last 2 rows twice more, then 2nd row again. 165(175-183) sts. Cast off in rib.

Lower Right Front and Vent Edging

Using circular needle and with right side facing, pick up and knit 54 sts down side edge of right front from cast on sts to lower edge, then 79(87-93) sts along cast on edge.

133(141-147) sts.

Turning at end of each row continue as follows.

1st row: [P1, k1] 3 times, work [p1, k1, p1] into next st, *k1, [p1, k1] twice, work [p1, k1, p1] into next st; rep from * 10(11-12) times more, [k1, p1] 2(3-3) times, k1, p1 (mark this st with a contrasting thread), [k1, p1] 27 times. 157(167-175) sts.

Complete as given for Lower Left Front and Vent Edging. Join shoulder seams.

Armbands

Using smaller needles and with right side facing, pick up and k179(189-199) sts around armhole opening.

1st row (wrong side): P1, *k1, p1; rep from * to end.

2nd row: K1, *p1, k1; rep from * to end.

Work 5 more rows in rib. Cast off in rib.

Button Band

Using smaller needles, cast on 11 sts. Starting with the 2nd row, work in k1, p1 rib as given for Armbands until band when slightly stretched fits up front edge (including lower edging) and around to centre of back neck. Cast off in rib. Sew band in place stretching evenly. Mark positions for 4 buttons, the top one level with first neck dec and the remainder spaced below, 7 cm [2 3/4 ins] apart.

Buttonhole Band

Work as given for Button Band **at the same time** working buttonholes to match markers on right side rows as follows:

Next row: Rib 4, cast off 2 sts, rib to end.

Next row: Rib to end casting on 2 sts over buttonhole.

Sew band in place and join at centre back. Sew side edges of vents in place to cast on sts. Join side seam from top of vent including edges of armbands. Sew on buttons.

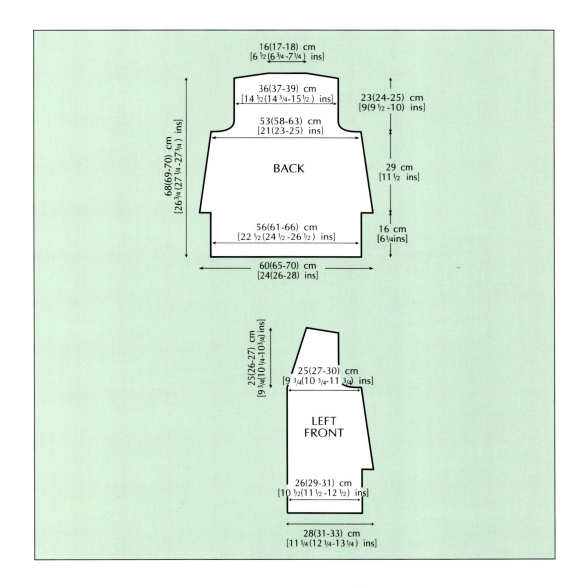

Lace Patterns

Arrowhead Lace

Multiple of 10 sts + 11.

1st row (right side): K1, *[yf, sl 1, k1, psso] twice, k1, [k2tog, yf] twice, k1; rep from * to end.

2nd row: Purl.

3rd row: K2, *yf, sl 1, k1, psso, yf, sl 1, k2tog, psso, yf, k2tog, yf, k3; rep from * to last 9 sts, yf, sl 1, k1, psso, yf, sl 1, k2tog, psso, yf, k2tog, yf, k2.

4th row: Purl.

Rep these 4 rows.

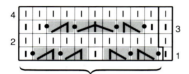

Rep these 10 sts

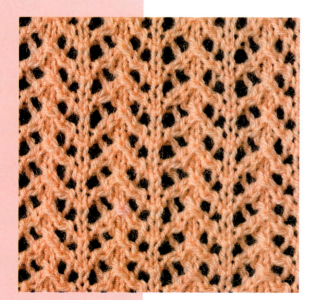

Little Arrowhead

Multiple of 6 sts + 7.

1st row (right side): K1, *yf, sl 1, k1, psso, k1, k2tog, yf, k1; rep from * to end.

2nd row: Purl.

3rd row: K2, *yf, sl 1, k2tog, psso, yf, k3; rep from * to last 5 sts, yf, sl 1, k2tog, psso, yf, k2.

4th row: Purl.

Rep these 4 rows.

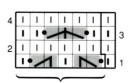

Rep these 6 sts

Lace Patterns

Feather Openwork

Multiple of 5 sts + 2.

1st row (right side): K1, *k2tog, yf, k1, yf, sl 1, k1, psso; rep from * to last st, k1.

2nd row: Purl.

Rep these 2 rows.

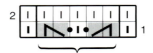

Rep these 5 sts

Chevron and Feather

Multiple of 13 sts + 2.

1st row (right side): K1, *sl 1, k1, psso, k4, yf, k1, yf, k4, k2tog; rep from * to last st, k1.

2nd row: Purl.

Rep these 2 rows.

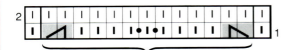

Rep these 13 sts

Lace Panels

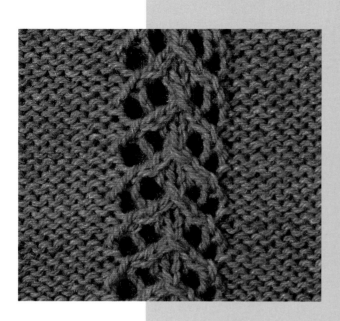

Lace Rib Panel

Panel of 7 sts on a background of reverse st st.

1st row (right side): P1, yon, sl 1, k1, psso, k1, k2tog, yfrn, p1.

2nd row: K1, p5, k1.

3rd row: P1, k1, yf, sl 1, k2tog, psso, yf, k1, p1.

4th row: K1, p5, k1.

Rep these 4 rows.

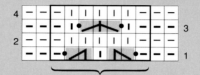

Panel of 7 sts

Faggoted Panel

Panel of 9 sts on a background of st st.

1st row (right side): P1, k1, k2tog, yf, k1, yf, k2togtbl, k1, p1.

2nd row: K1, p7, k1.

3rd row: P1, k2tog, yf, k3, yf, k2togtbl, p1.

4th row: K1, p7, k1.

Rep these 4 rows.

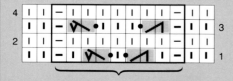

Panel of 9 sts

Lace Panels

Vandyke Lace Panel

Panel of 17 sts on a background of st st.

1st row (right side): *K2tog, yf, k1, yf, sl 1, k1, psso*, k3, yf, sl 1, k1, psso, k2; rep from * to * once more.

2nd row: P17.

3rd row: [K2tog, yf, k1, yf, sl 1, k1, psso, k1] twice, k2tog, yf, k1, yf, sl 1, k1, psso.

4th row: P17.

5th row: *K2tog, yf, k1, yf, sl 1, k1, psso*, k2tog, yf, k3, yf, sl 1, k1, psso; rep from * to * once more.

6th row: P17.

Rep these 6 rows.

Diamond Panel

Panel of 11 sts on a background of st st.

1st row (right side): P2, k2tog, [k1, yf] twice, k1, sl 1, k1, psso, p2.

2nd and every alt row: K2, p7, k2.

3rd row: P2, k2tog, yf, k3, yf, sl 1, k1, psso, p2.

5th row: P2, k1, yf, sl 1, k1, psso, k1, k2tog, yf, k1, p2.

7th row: P2, k2, yf, sl 1, k2tog, psso, yf, k2, p2.

8th row: K2, p7, k2.

Rep these 8 rows.

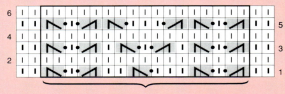

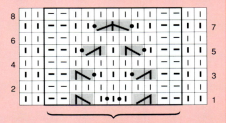

29

His and Her Guernsey Sweater

Measurements

To fit bust/chest size	75/80	85/90	95/100	cm
	30/32	34/36	38/40	ins
Finished measurement	97	107	117	cm
	39	43	47	ins
Length to shoulder	63	63	63	cm
(approximately)	25	25	25	ins
Sleeve length	44	45	46	cm
(approximately)	17½	18	18½	ins

Shown in 75/80 cm [30/32 inch] and 95/100 cm [38/40 inch] sizes.

Materials

Double Knitting yarn 850 900 1000 grams
30 32 36 ounces

Pair needles each size 3¼mm (UK 10, USA 3 or 4) and 4mm (UK 8, USA 6). Cable needle.

The quantities of yarn stated are based on average requirements and are therefore approximate.
For abbreviations see pages 19 and 20.

Tension

22 sts and 30 rows = 10 cm [4 ins] square measured over st st using larger needles.

Special Abbreviation

C5R (Cable 5 Right) = slip next 2 sts on to cable needle and hold at back of work, knit next 3 sts from left-hand needle, then knit sts from cable needle.

Panel A (11 sts)

1st row (right side): K5, p1, k5.
2nd row: P4, k3, p4.
3rd row: K3, p2, k1, p2, k3.
4th row: P2, k2, p3, k2, p2.
5th row: K1, p2, k5, p2, k1.
6th row: P2, k2, p3, k2, p2.
7th row: K3, p2, k1, p2, k3.
8th row: P4, k3, p4.
9th row: K5, p1, k5.
10th row: P11.
These 10 rows form panel A.

Panel B (11 sts)

1st row (right side): K5, p1, k5.
2nd row: P4, k1, p1, k1, p4.
3rd row: K3, [p1, k3] twice.
4th row: P2, k1, p5, k1, p2.
5th row: K1, p1, k7, p1, k1.
6th row: P5, k1, p5.
7th row: K4, p1, k1, p1, k4.
8th row: P3, [k1, p3] twice.
9th row: K2, p1, k5, p1, k2.
10th row: P1, k1, p7, k1, p1.
These 10 rows form panel B.

Panel C (29 sts)

1st row (right side): P2, k2, p8, k1, [p1, k1] twice, p8, k2, p2.
2nd row: K2, p3, k7, p5, k7, p3, k2.
3rd row: K6, p6, k1, [p1, k1] twice, p6, k6.
4th row: P7, k5, p5, k5, p7.
5th row: P2, k6, p4, k1, [p1, k1] twice, p4, k6, p2.
6th row: K2, p7, k3, p5, k3, p7, k2.
7th row: K10, p2, k1, [p1, k1] twice, p2, k10.
8th row: P11, k1, p5, k1, p11.
These 8 rows form panel C.

Panel D (11 sts)

1st row (right side): K6, p1, k2, p1, k1.
2nd row: [P2, k1] twice, p5.
3rd row: K4, p1, k2, p1, k3.
4th row: P4, k1, p2, k1, p3.
5th row: [K2, p1] twice, k5.
6th row: P6, k1, p2, k1, p1.
7th row: [K2, p1] twice, k5.
8th row: P4, k1, p2, k1, p3.
9th row: K4, p1, k2, p1, k3.
10th row: [P2, k1] twice, p5.
These 10 rows form panel D.

Panel E (11 sts)

1st row (right side): K11.
2nd row: P11.
3rd row: K11.
4th row: P11.
5th row: K5, p1, k5.
6th row: P4, k1, p1, k1, p4.
7th row: K3, p1, [k1, p1] twice, k3.
8th row: P2, k1, p5, k1, p2.
9th row: K1, p1, [k3, p1] twice, k1.
10th row: P1, k1, p7, k1, p1.
11th row: K5, p1, k5.
12th row: P11.
13th row: K5, p1, k5.
14th row: P11.
15th row: K3, p5, k3.
16th row: P5, k1, p5.
17th row: K3, p5, k3.
18th row: P11.
19th row: K5, p1, k5.
20th row: P11.
21st row: K5, p1, k5.
22nd row: P4, k1, p1, k1, p4.
23rd row: K3, [p1, k1] twice, p1, k3.
24th row: P4, k1, p1, k1, p4.
25th row: K5, p1, k5.
26th row: P11.
These 26 rows form panel E.

Panel F (15 sts)

1st row (right side): K7, p1, k7.
2nd row: P6, k1, p1, k1, p6.
3rd row: K5, p1, k3, p1, k5.
4th row: P4, k1, [p2, k1] twice, p4.
5th row: K3, p1, k2, p1, k1, p1, k2, p1, k3.
6th row: [P2, k1] twice, p3, [k1, p2] twice.
7th row: K1, [p1, k2] 4 times, p1, k1.
8th row: P3, k1, p2, k1, p1, k1, p2, k1, p3.
9th row: [K2, p1] twice, k3, [p1, k2] twice.
10th row: P4, k1, [p2, k1] twice, p4.
11th row: K3, p1, k2, p1, k1, p1, k2, p1, k3.
12th row: P5, k1, p3, k1, p5.
13th row: K4, p1, [k2, p1] twice, k4.
14th row: P6, k1, p1, k1, p6.
15th row: K5, p1, k3, p1, k5.
16th row: P7, k1, p7.
17th row: K6, p1, k1, p1, k6.
18th row: P15.
19th row: K7, p1, k7.
20th row: P15.
21st row: K15.
22nd row: P15.
23rd row: K1, p13, k1.
24th row: P15.
25th row: K1, p13, k1.
26th row: P15.
27th row: K15.
28th row: P15.
These 28 rows form panel F.

His and Her Guernsey Sweater

Front

Using smaller needles, cast on 90(102-114) sts.

1st row (right side): K2, *p2, k2; rep from * to end.

2nd row: P2, *k2, p2; rep from * to end.

Rep these 2 rows until rib measures 8 cm [3 ins], ending with a right side row.

Next row (increase): Rib 5(6-7), *inc in next st, rib 1, inc in next st, rib 2; rep from * to last 5(6-7) sts, inc in next st, rib to end. 123(139-155) sts.

Change to larger needles.

Commence first pattern.

1st row (right side): [K1, p1] 0(4-8) times, work 1st row of panel A across next 11 sts, p1, [k1, p1] 3 times, work 1st row of panel B across next 11 sts, p1, [k1, p1] 3 times, work 1st row of panel A across next 11 sts, work 1st row of panel C across next 29 sts, work 1st row of panel A across next 11 sts, p1, [k1, p1] 3 times, work 1st row of panel B across next 11 sts, p1, [k1, p1] 3 times, work 1st row of panel A across next 11 sts, [p1, k1] 0(4-8) times.

2nd row: [P1, k3] 0(2-4) times, work 2nd row of panel A, k3, p1, k3, work 2nd row of panel B, k3, p1, k3, work 2nd row of panel A, work 2nd of panel C, of panel A, k3, p1, k3, work 2nd row of panel B, k3, p1, k3, work 2nd row of panel A, [k3, p1] 0(2-4) times.

These 2 rows set the position of panels and form pattern at each side and between panels.

Continue in pattern as set, **working appropriate rows of panels** until front measures approximately 34 cm [13½ ins], ending with 9th row of panels A and B, and 7th row of panel C.

1st and 2nd sizes only

Next row (decrease): P1(6), *p2tog, p8(5); rep from * to last 2(0) sts, [p2tog] 1(0) time.

3rd size only

Next row (decrease): P3, * p2tog, p9, p2tog, p8; rep from * to last 5 sts, p2tog, p3.

All sizes: 110(120-140) sts remain.

Commence second pattern.

1st row (right side): Purl.

2nd row: Knit.

3rd row: Purl.

4th row: *K2, p8; rep from * to end.

5th row: *K7, p2, k1; rep from * to end.

6th row: *P2, k2, p6; rep from * to end.

7th row: *K5, p2, k3; rep from * to end.

8th row: *P4, k2, p4; rep from * to end.

9th row: *K3, p2, k5; rep from * to end.

10th row: *P6, k2, p2; rep from * to end.

11th row: *K1, p2, k7; rep from * to end.

12th row: *P8, k2; rep from * to end.

13th row: Purl.

14th row: Knit.

15th row: *P2, k8; rep from * to end.

16th row: *P7, k2, p1; rep from * to end.

17th row: *K2, p2, k6; rep from * to end.

18th row: *P5, k2, p3; rep from * to end.

19th row: *K4, p2, k4; rep from * to end.

20th row: *P3, k2, p5; rep from * to end.

21st row: *K6, p2, k2; rep from * to end.

22nd row: *P1, k2, p7; rep from * to end.

23rd row: *K8, p2; rep from * to end.

24th row: Knit.

25th row: Purl.

26th row: Knit.

Next row (increase): K7(5-10), *inc in next st, k7(4-5); rep from * to last 7(5-10) sts, inc in next st, knit to end. 123(143-161) sts.

Next row: Purl.

Commence third pattern.

1st row (right side): K0(0-1), [p1, k1] 0(0-4) times, [p2, k5, p2, k1] 0(1-1) time, p1, k1, p1, work 1st row of panel D across next 11 sts, p1, k1, p1, work 1st row of panel E across next 11 sts, p1, k1, p1, k7, p2, k5, p2, k1, p2, k2, p2, work 1st row of panel F across next 15 sts, p2, k2, p2, k1, p2, k5, p2, k7, p1, k1, p1, work 1st row of panel E across next 11 sts, p1, k1, p1, work 1st row of panel D across next 11 sts, p1, k1, p1, [k1, p2, k5, p2] 0(1-1) time, [k1, p1] 0(0-4) times, k0(0-1).

2nd row: P0(0-1), [k3, p1] 0(0-2) times, [k2, p5, k2, p1] 0(1-1) time, k3, work 2nd row of panel D, k3, work 2nd row of panel E, k3, p7, k2, p5, k2, p1, k2, p2, k2, work 2nd row of panel F, k2, p2, k2, p1, k2, p5, k2, p7, k3, work 2nd row of panel E, k3, work 2nd row of panel D, k3, [p1, k2, p5, k2] 0(1-1) time, [p1, K3] 0(0-2) times, p0(0-1).

3rd row: K0(0-1), [p1, k1] 0(0-4) times, [p2, C5R, p2, k1] 0(1,1) time, p1, k1, p1, work 3rd row of panel D, p1, k1, p1, work 3rd row of panel E, p1, k1, p1, k7, p2, C5R, p2, k3, p2, k2, work 3rd row of panel F, k2, p2, k3, p2, C5R, p2, k7, p1, k1, p1, work 3rd row of panel E, p1, k1, p1, work 3rd row of panel D, p1, k1, p1, [k1, p2, C5R, p2] 0(1-1) time, [k1, p1] 0(0-4) times, k0(0-1).

4th row: P0(0-1), [k3, p1] 0(0-2) times, [k2, p5, k2, p1] 0(1-1) time, k3, work 4th row of panel D, k3, work 4th row of panel E, k3, p7, k2, p5, k2, p3, k2, p2, work 4th row of panel F, p2, k2, p3, k2, p5, k2, p7, k3, work 4th row of panel E, k3, work 4th row of panel D, k3, [p1, k2, p5, k2] 0(1-1) time, [p1, k3] 0(0-2) times, p0(0-1).

5th row: K0(0-1), [p1, k1] 0(0-4) times, [p2, k5, p2, k1] 0(1-1) time, p1, k1, p1, work 5th row of panel D, p1, k1, p1, work 5th row of panel E, p1, k1, p1, k7, p2, k5, p2, k1, p2, k2, p2, work 5th row of panel F, p2, k2, p2, k1, p2, k5, p2, k7, p1, k1, p1, work 5th row of panel E, p1, k1, p1, work 5th row of panel D, p1, k1, p1, [k1, p2, k5, p2] 0(1-1) time, [k1, p1] 0(0-4) times, k0(0-1).

6th row: P0(0-1), [k3, p1] 0(0-2) times, [k2, p5, k2, p1] 0(1-1) time, k3, work 6th row of panel D, k3, work 6th row of panel E, k3, p1, k5, p1, k2, p5, k2, p1, k2, p2, k2, work 6th row of panel F, k2, p2, k2, p1, k2, p5, k2, p1, k5, p1, k3, work 6th row of panel E, k3, work 6th row of panel D, k3, [p1, k2, p5, k2] 0(1-1) time, [p1, k3] 0(0-2) times, p0(0-1).

7th row: K0(0-1), [p1, k1] 0(0-4) times, [p2, k5, p2, k1] 0(1-1) time, p1, k1, p1, work 7th row of panel D, p1, k1, p1, work 7th row of panel E, p1, k1, p1, k7, p2, k5, p2, k3, p2, k2, work 7th row of panel F, k2, p2, k3, p2, k5, p2, k7, p1, k1, p1, work 7th row of panel E, p1, k1, p1, work 7th row of panel D, p1, k1, p1, [k1, p2, k5, p2] 0(1-1) time, [k1, p1] 0(0-4) times, k0(0-1).

8th row: P0(0-1), [k3, p1] 0(0-2) times, [k2, p5, k2, p1] 0(1,1) time, k3, work 8th row of panel D, k3, work 8th row of panel E, k3, p7, k2, p5, k2, p3, k2, p2, work 8th row of panel F, p2, k2, p3, k2, p5, k2, p7, k3, work 8th row of panel E, k3, work 8th row of panel D, k3, [p1, k2, p5, k2] 0(1-1) time, [p1, k3] 0(0-2) times, p0(0-1).

These 8 rows set the position of panels and form pattern at each side and between panels ★.

Continue in pattern as set, **working appropriate rows of panels** until front measures approximately 56 cm [22 ins], ending with 8th row of panel D, 22nd row of panel E and 20th row of panel F.

Shape Neck

Next row: Work 50(60-69) sts in pattern, turn and complete this side first.

Keeping pattern correct, dec 1 st at neck edge on next 6 rows, then on following 5 alt rows. 39(49-58) sts remain. Work 7 rows straight (work 1 row more here for 2nd side), thus ending at side edge.

Shape Shoulder

Cast off 19(24-29) sts at beg of next row. Work 1 row. Cast off remaining 20(25-29) sts.

With right side facing, slip centre 23 sts onto a holder, rejoin yarn to remaining 50(60-69) sts, work in pattern to end. Complete to match first side, reversing shapings, by working 1 row more where indicated.

Back

Work as given for Front to ★. Continue in pattern as set, **working appropriate rows of panels** until back measures same as front to start of shoulder shaping, ending with a wrong side row.

Shape Shoulders

Cast off 19(24-29) sts at beg of next 2 rows, then 20(25-29) sts at beg of following 2 rows. Slip remaining 45 sts on to a holder.

Sleeves

With smaller needles, cast on 46(50-50) sts and work in k2, p2 rib as given for Front until rib measures 4(5-6) cm [1 1/2(2-2 1/2) ins] ending with a right side row.

Next row (increase): Rib 1(3-3), * inc in each of next 3(2-2) sts, rib 1; rep from * to last 5 sts, inc in each of next 3(1-1) sts, rib to end. 79 sts. Change to larger needles and commence pattern.

1st row (right side): [K1, p1] twice, work 1st row of panel B across next 11 sts, p1, k1, p1, work 1st row of panel A across next 11 sts, p1, k1, p1, work 1st row of panel F across next 15 sts, p1, k1, p1, work 1st row of panel A across next 11 sts, p1, k1, p1, work 1st row of panel B across next 11 sts, [p1, k1] twice.

2nd row: P1, k3, work 2nd row of panel B, k3, work 2nd row of panel A, k3, work 2nd row of panel F, k3, work 2nd row of panel A, k3, work 2nd row of panel B, k3, p1.

These 2 rows set the position of panels and form pattern at each side and between panels.

Continue in pattern as set, **working appropriate rows of panels,** and bringing extra sts into side pattern, inc 1 st at each end of next and every following 4th(4th-alt) row until there are 119(139-89) sts.

1st and 3nd sizes only: Inc 1 st at each end of every following 6th(4th) row until there are 131(143) sts.

All sizes: Work 15(11-11) rows straight, thus ending with a wrong side row. Cast off loosely.

Finishing and Neckband

Block, but do not press. Join right shoulder seam.

Neckband

Using smaller needles and with right side of work facing, pick up and k26 sts down left front slope, work across 23 sts on holder at front neck decreasing 1 st at centre, pick up and k26 sts up right front slope, then work across 45 sts on holder at back neck decreasing 1 st at centre. 118 sts.

Next row (wrong side): Knit.

Next row: Purl.

Next row: Purl.

Starting with 1st row, work 8 rows in k2, p2 rib as given for Front.

Next row: K2, *k2togtbl, k2; rep from * to end. 89 sts remain.

Next row: Knit.

Next row: Purl.

Cast off knitwise.

Join left shoulder seam and ends of neckband.

Fold each sleeve in half lengthways and mark centre of cast off edge.

Sew each sleeve to a side edge placing centre at shoulder seam. Join side and sleeve seams.

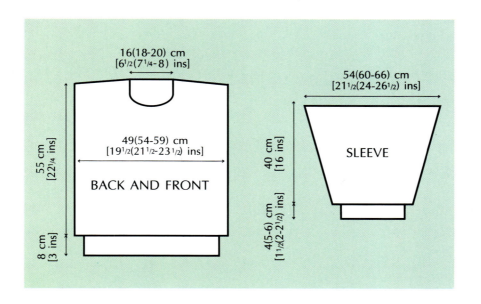

Knit and Purl Textures

Box and Stripe Pattern

Multiple of 6 sts + 3.

1st row (right side): Knit.

2nd row: Knit.

3rd and 4th rows: Rep these 2 rows once more.

5th row: Knit.

6th row: K3, *p3, k3; rep from * to end.

7th and 8th rows: Rep the last 2 rows once more.

9th to 12th rows: Rep 1st and 2nd rows twice.

13th row: Knit.

14th row: P3, *k3, p3; rep from * to end.

15th and 16th rows: Rep the last 2 rows once more.

Rep these 16 rows.

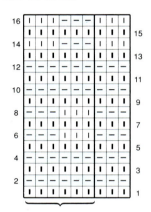

Rep these 6 sts

Track Pattern

Multiple of 12 sts + 17.

1st row (right side): K5, *p3, k1, p3, k5; rep from * to end.

2nd row: K8, p1, *k11, p1; rep from * to last 8 sts, k8.

3rd and 4th rows: Rep these 2 rows once more.

5th row: K5, *p2, k1, p1, k1, p2, k5; rep from * to end.

6th row: K7, p1, k1, p1, *k9, p1, k1, p1; rep from * to last 7 sts, k7.

7th and 8th rows: Rep the last 2 rows once more.

Rep these 8 rows.

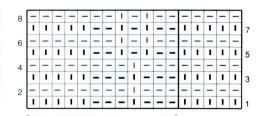

Rep these 12 sts

Knit and Purl Textures

Large Basket Weave

Multiple of 6 sts + 8.

1st row (right side): Knit.

2nd row: Purl.

3rd row: K2, *p4, k2; rep from * to end.

4th row: P2, *k4, p2; rep from * to end.

5th and 6th rows: Rep the last 2 rows once more.

7th and 8th rows: As 1st and 2nd rows.

9th row: P3, *k2, p4; rep from * to last 5 sts, k2, p3.

10th row: K3, *p2, k4; rep from * to last 5 sts, p2, k3.

11th and 12th rows: Rep the last 2 rows once more.

Rep these 12 rows.

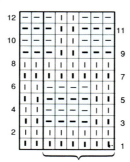

Rep these 6 sts

Ladder Stitch

Multiple of 8 sts + 5.

1st row (right side): K5, *p3, k5; rep from * to end.

2nd row: P5, *k3, p5; rep from * to end.

3rd and 4th rows: Rep these 2 rows once more.

5th row: K1, p3, *k5, p3; rep from * to last st, k1.

6th row: P1, k3, *p5, k3; rep from * to last st, p1.

7th and 8th rows: Rep the last 2 rows once more.

Rep these 8 rows.

Rep these 8 sts

Knit and Purl Patterns

Polperro Horizontal Diamonds

Multiple of 12 sts + 13.

1st row (right side): Knit.

2nd row: Purl.

3rd row: Knit.

4th row: Knit.

5th to 8th rows: Rep 1st and 2nd rows twice.

9th row: K6, p1, *k11, p1; rep from * to last 6 sts, k6.

10th row: P5, k1, p1, k1, *p9, k1, p1, k1; rep from * to last 5 sts, p5.

11th row: K4, p1, k3, p1, *k7, p1, k3, p1; rep from * to last 4 sts, k4.

12th row: P3, k1, *p5, k1; rep from * to last 3 sts, p3.

13th row: K2, p1, k7, p1, *k3, p1, k7, p1; rep from * to last 2 sts, k2.

14th row: P1, *k1, p9, k1, p1; rep from * to end.

15th row: P1, *k11, p1; rep from * to end.

16th row: As 14th row.

17th row: As 13th row.

18th row: As 12th row.

19th row: As 11th row.

20th row: As 10th row.

21st row: As 9th row.

22nd row: Purl.

Rep these 22 rows.

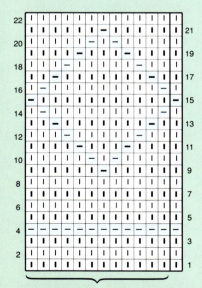

Rep these 12 sts

Knit and Purl Panels

Marriage Lines

Panel of 17 sts on a background of st st.

1st row (right side): P3, k6, p1, k2, p1, k1, p3.

2nd row: K1, p1, [k1, p2] twice, k1, p5, k1, p1, k1.

3rd row: P3, k4, p1, k2, p1, k3, p3.

4th row: K1, p1, k1, p4, k1, p2, k1, p3, k1, p1, k1.

5th row: P3, [k2, p1] twice, k5, p3.

6th row: K1, p1, k1, p6, k1, p2, [k1, p1] twice, k1.

7th row: As 5th row.

8th row: As 4th row.

9th row: As 3rd row.

10th row: As 2nd row.

Rep these 10 rows.

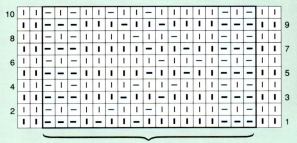

Panel of 17 sts

Ridge and Furrow

Panel of 23 sts on a background of st st.

1st row (right side): P4, k7, p1, k7, p4.

2nd row: K1, p2, k1, p5, [k1, p1] twice, k1, p5, k1, p2, k1.

3rd row: P4, k4, [p1, k2] twice, p1, k4, p4.

4th row: K1, p2, [k1, p3] 4 times, k1, p2, k1.

5th row: P4, k2, [p1, k4] twice, p1, k2, p4.

6th row: K1, p2, k1, p1, [k1, p5] twice, k1, p1, k1, p2, k1.

Rep these 6 rows.

Panel of 23 sts

Knit and Purl Panels

Ladder

Panel of 11 sts on a background of st st.

1st row (right side): P2, k7, p2.

2nd row: K2, p7, k2.

3rd and 4th rows: Rep these 2 rows once more.

5th row: Purl.

6th row: K2, p7, k2.

7th row: P2, k7, p2.

8th and 9th rows: Rep the last 2 rows once more.

10th row: Knit.

Rep these 10 rows.

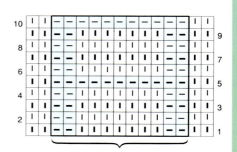

Panel of 11 sts

Triple Wave

Panel of 14 sts on a background of st st.

1st row (right side): P3, k8, p3.

2nd row: [K1, p1] twice, k2, p2, k2, [p1, k1] twice.

3rd row: P3, k3, p2, k3, p3.

4th row: K1, p1, k1, p8, k1, p1, k1.

5th row: P3, k1, p2, k2, p2, k1, p3.

6th row: K1, p1, k1, p3, k2, p3, k1, p1, k1.

Rep these 6 rows.

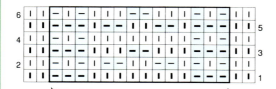

Panel of 14 sts

Knit and Purl Panels

Diamond Net Mask

Panel of 19 sts on a background of st st.

1st row (right side): P3, k6, p1, k6, p3.

2nd row: K1, p1, k1, [p6, k1] twice, p1, k1.

3rd row: P3, k5, p1, k1, p1, k5, p3.

4th row: K1, p1, k1, [p5, k1, p1, k1] twice.

5th row: P3, k4, [p1, k1] twice, p1, k4, p3.

6th row: K1, p1, k1, p4, [k1, p1] twice, k1, p4, k1, p1, k1.

7th row: P3, k3, [p1, k1] 3 times, p1, k3, p3.

8th row: K1, p1, k1, p3, [k1, p1] 3 times, k1, p3, k1, p1, k1.

9th row: P3, k2, p1, k1, p1, k3, p1, k1, p1, k2, p3.

10th row: K1, p1, k1, p2, k1, p1, k1, p3, k1, p1, k1, p2, k1, p1, k1.

11th row: P3, [k1, p1] twice, k5, [p1, k1] twice, p3.

12th row: [K1, p1] 3 times, k1, p5, [k1, p1] 3 times, k1.

13th and 14th rows: As 9th and 10th rows.

15th and 16th rows: As 7th and 8th rows.

17th and 18th rows: As 5th and 6th rows.

19th and 20th rows: As 3rd and 4th rows.

Rep these 20 rows.

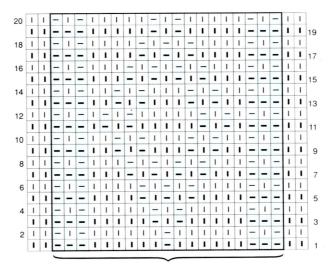

Panel of 19 sts

Cabled Dress

Measurements

To fit bust size	75-85	90-100	cm
	30-34	36-40	ins
Finished measurement	97	112	cm
	39	45	ins
Length to back neck (approximately)	90	90	cm
	36	36	ins
Sleeve length (approximately)	40	40	cm
	16	16	ins

Shown in 75-85 cm [30-34 inch] size.

Materials

Double Knitting yarn	1050	1150	grams
	38	42	ounces

Pair needles each size 3¼ (UK 10, USA 3 or 4) and 4mm (UK 8, USA 6). Circular needles each size 3¼mm (UK 10, USA 3 or 4) and 4mm (UK 8, USA 6) 60 cm [24 ins] long and circular needle size 4mm (UK 8, USA 6) 80 cm [30 ins] long.

The quantities of yarn stated are based on average requirements and are therefore approximate.
For abbreviations see pages 19 and 20.

Tension

22 sts and 30 rows = 10 cm [4 ins] square measured over st st using larger needles.

Special Abbreviations

KB1 or PB1 = knit or purl into back of st.

C4B (Cable 4 Back) = slip next 2 sts on to cable needle and hold at back of work, knit next 2 sts from left-hand needle, then knit sts from cable needle.

C4F (Cable 4 Front) = slip next 2 sts on to cable needle and hold at front of work, knit next 2 sts from left-hand needle, then knit sts from cable needle.

C6B (Cable 6 Back) = slip next 3 sts on to cable needle and hold at back of work, knit next 3 sts from left-hand needle, then knit sts from cable needle.

C8B (Cable 8 Back) = slip next 4 sts on to cable needle and hold at back of work, knit next 4 sts from left-hand needle, then knit sts from cable needle.

C8F (Cable 8 Front) = slip next 4 sts on to cable needle and hold at front of work, knit next 4 sts from left-hand needle, then knit sts from cable needle.

Back and Front (Alike)

Using pair of smaller needles cast on 111(125) sts.

1st row (right side): KB1, *p1, KB1; rep from * to end.

2nd row: PB1, *k1, PB1; rep from * to end.

Rep these 2 rows until rib measures 4 cm [1½ ins] ending with a right side row.

Next row (increase): Rib 3(4), *inc in next st, rib 1; rep from * to last 4(5) sts, inc in next st, rib to end. 164(184) sts.

Change to pair of larger needles and commence pattern.

1st row: [KB1, p1] 5(6) times, k12, *p1, [KB1, p1] 10(12) times, k12; rep from * to last 10(12) sts, [p1, KB1] 5(6) times.

2nd row: [PB1, k1] 5(6) times, p12, *k1, [PB1, k1] 10(12) times, p12; rep from * to last 10(12) sts, [k1, PB1] 5(6) times.

3rd row: [KB1, p1] 5(6) times, k4, C8B, *p1, [KB1, p1] 10(12) times, k4, C8B; rep from * to last 10(12) sts, [p1, KB1] 5(6) times.

4th row: As 2nd row.

5th row: As 1st row.

6th row: As 2nd row.

7th row: [KB1, p1] 5(6) times, C8F, k4, *p1, [KB1, p1] 10(12) times, C8F, k4; rep from * to last 10(12) sts, [p1, KB1] 5(6) times.

8th row: As 2nd row.

These 8 rows form the pattern. Continue in pattern until piece measures approximately 59 cm [23½ ins] ending with a 5th row of pattern.

Next row: Cast off 8(10) sts, work to last 8(10) sts, cast off last 8(10) sts. Slip remaining 148(164) sts on to a holder for yoke.

Sleeves

Using pair of smaller needles cast on 55(61) sts and work 4 cm [1½ ins] in rib as given for Back and Front ending with a right side row.

Next row (increase): Rib 3(5), *inc in each of next 2 sts, rib 1; rep from * to last 4(5) sts, inc in next st, rib to end. 88(96) sts.

Change to pair of larger needles and commence pattern.

1st row: [P1, KB1] twice, p1, k12, *p1, [KB1, p1] 10(12) times, k12; rep from * once more, p1, [KB1, p1] twice.

2nd row: [K1, PB1] twice, k1, p12, *k1, [PB1, k1] 10(12) times, p12; rep from * once more, k1, [PB1, k1] twice.

3rd row: [P1, KB1] twice, p1, k4, C8B, *p1, [KB1, p1] 10(12) times, k4, C8B; rep from * once more, p1, [KB1, p1] twice.

4th row: As 2nd row.

5th row: As 1st row.

6th row: As 2nd row.

7th row: [P1, KB1] twice, p1, C8F, k4, *p1, [KB1, p1] 10(12) times, C8F, k4; rep from * once more, p1, [KB1, p1] twice.

8th row: As 2nd row.

Keeping pattern correct and bringing extra sts into rib pattern, inc 1 st at each end of next and every following 4th(3rd) row until there are 110(124) sts, then every following 5th(4th) row until there are 132(152) sts. Work 5 rows straight thus ending with a 5th row of pattern.

Next row: Cast off 8(10) sts, work to last 8(10) sts, cast off last 8(10) sts. Slip remaining 116(132) sts on to a holder for yoke.

Cabled Dress

Yoke

Using 80 cm [30 ins] circular needle and with right side of each piece facing, work in pattern across sts of back, one sleeve, front, then 2nd sleeve. 528(592) sts.

Join into a ring, place a marker to mark beg of rounds. Working in rounds (every row is a right side row, therefore 2nd, 4th, 6th and 8th rows of pattern are now the same as 1st row), work 25 rounds in pattern as set thus ending with an 8th row of pattern.

Shape Yoke

Note: To avoid stretching work, use a shorter length circular needle when necessary.

1st round (decrease): Work 35(39) sts, k2tog, [k3, k2tog] twice, *work 54(62) sts, k2tog, [k3, k2tog] twice; rep from * to last 19(23) sts, work to end. 504(568) sts remain.

2nd round: Work 35(39) sts, k9, *work 54(62) sts, k9; rep from * to last 19(23) sts, work to end.

3rd round: KB1, p1, k4, C8B, p1, [KB1, p1] 10(12) times, k3, C6B, *p1, [KB1, p1] 10(12) times, k4, C8B, p1, [KB1, p1] 10(12) times, k3, C6B; rep from * to last 19(23) sts, p1, [KB1, p1] 9(11) times.

4th round: As 2nd round.

5th round (decrease): Work 35(39) sts, k2tog, k1, k2tog, k2, k2tog, *work 54(62) sts, k2tog, k1, k2tog, k2, k2tog; rep from * to last 19(23) sts, work to end. 480(544) sts remain.

6th round: Work 35(39) sts, k6, *work 54(62) sts, k6; rep from * to last 19(23) sts, work to end.

7th round: KB1, p1, C8F, k4, p1, [KB1, p1] 10(12) times, C4F, k2, *p1, [KB1, p1] 10(12) times, C8F, k4, p1, [KB1, p1] 10(12) times, C4F, k2; rep from * to last 19(23) sts, p1, [KB1, p1] 9(11) times.

8th round: As 6th round.

9th round (decrease): Work 35(39) sts, [k2tog] 3 times, *work 54(62) sts, [k2tog] 3 times; rep from * to last 19(23) sts, work to end. 456(520) sts remain.

10th round: Work 35(39) sts, k3, *work 54(62) sts, k3; rep from * to last 19(23) sts, work to end.

11th round (decrease): KB1, p1, k4, C8B, p1, [KB1, p1] 10(12) times, sl 2tog, k1, p2sso (see Special Abbreviations on page 20), *p1, [KB1, p1] 10(12) times, k4, C8B, p1, [KB1, p1] 10(12) times, sl 2tog, k1, p2sso; rep from * to last 19(23) sts, p1, [KB1, p1] 9(11) times. 440(504) sts remain.

12th and 13th rounds: KB1, p1, k12, *p1, [KB1, p1] 21(25) times, k12; rep from * to last 41(49) sts, p1, [KB1, p1] 20(24) times.

14th round (decrease): KB1, p1, k12, [p1, KB1] 10(12) times, sl 2tog, k1, p2sso, *[KB1, p1] 10(12) times, k12, [p1, KB1] 10(12) times, sl 2tog, k1, p2sso; rep from * to last 18(22) sts, [KB1, p1] 9(11) times. 424(488) sts remain.

15th round: KB1, p1, C8F, k4, p1, [KB1, p1] 9(11) times, [KB1] 3 times, *p1, [KB1, p1] 9(11) times, C8F, k4, p1, [KB1, p1] 9(11) times, [KB1] 3 times; rep from * to last 17(21) sts, p1, [KB1, p1] 8(10) times.

16th round: KB1, p1, k12, p1, [KB1, p1] 9(11) times, [KB1] 3 times, *p1, [KB1, p1] 9(11) times, k12, p1, [KB1, p1] 9(11) times, [KB1] 3 times; rep from * to last 17(21) sts, p1, [KB1, p1] 8(10) times.

17th round (decrease): KB1, p1, k12, p1, [KB1, p1] 9(11) times, sl 2tog, k1, p2sso, *p1, [KB1, p1] 9(11) times, k12, p1, [KB1, p1] 9(11) times, sl 2tog, k1, p2sso; rep from * to last 17(21) sts, p1, [KB1, p1] 8(10) times. 408(472) sts remain.

18th round: KB1, p1, k12, *p1, [KB1, p1] 19(23) times, k12; rep from * to last 37(45) sts, p1, [KB1, p1] 18(22) times.

19th round: KB1, p1, k4, C4B, *p1, [KB1, p1] 19(23) times, k4, C8B; rep from * to last 37(45) sts, p1, [KB1, p1] 18(22) times.

20th round (decrease): KB1, p1, k12, [p1, KB1] 9(11) times, sl 2tog, k1, p2sso, *[KB1, p1] 9(11) times, k12, [p1, KB1] 9(11) times, sl 2tog, k1, p2sso; rep from * to last 16(20) sts, [KB1, p1] 8(10) times. 392(456) sts remain.

Keeping pattern correct, continue to dec 16 sts on every 3rd round in this way until 152(344) sts remain.

2nd size only: Decrease 16 sts as before on every alt row until 152 sts remain.

Both sizes: Work 1 round straight.

Neckband

Change to smaller circular needle and work 13 cm [5 ins] in pattern as set. Cast off loosely in pattern.

To Finish

Block, but do not press.

Fold neckband in half to inside and slip-stitch **loosely** in place. Join side, sleeve and underarm seams.

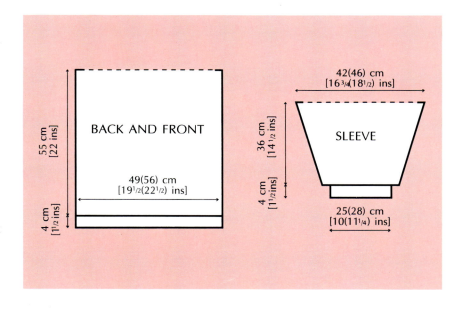

Rib Patterns

Woven Rib

Multiple of 6 sts + 3.

Note: Slip sts purlwise with yarn at front (right side) of work, on right side rows = ⌇ on chart.

1st row (right side): P3, *sl 1, yb, k1, yf, sl 1, p3; rep from * to end.

2nd row: K3, *p3, k3; rep from * to end.

3rd row: *P3, k1, yf, sl 1, yb, k1; rep from * to last 3 sts, p3.

4th row: As 2nd row.

Rep these 4 rows.

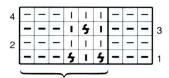

Rep these 6sts

Sailors Rib

Multiple of 5 sts + 3.

1st row (right side): P1, KB1, p1, *k2, p1, KB1, p1; rep from * to end.

2nd row: K1, p1, k1, *p2, k1, p1, k1; rep from * to end.

3rd row: P1, KB1, *p4, KB1; rep from * to last st, p1.

4th row: K1, p1, *k4, p1; rep from * to last st, k1.

Rep these 4 rows.

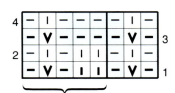

Rep these 5 sts

Rib Patterns

Interrupted Rib

Multiple of 2 sts + 1.

1st row (right side): P1, *k1, p1; rep from * to end.

2nd row: K1, *p1, k1; rep from * to end.

3rd row: Purl.

4th row: Knit.

Rep these 4 rows.

Rep these 2 sts

Double Twisted Rib

Multiple of 6 sts + 2.

1st row (right side): P2, *C2F, C2B, p2; rep from * to end.

2nd row: K2, *p4, k2; rep from * to end.

Rep these 2 rows.

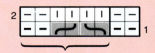

Rep these 6 sts

Rib Patterns

Shadow Rib

Multiple of 3 sts + 2.

1st row (right side): Knit.

2nd row: P2, *KB1, p2; rep from * to end.

Rep these 2 rows.

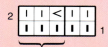

Rep these 3 sts

Feather Rib

Multiple of 5 sts + 2.

1st row (right side): P2, *yon, k2togtbl, k1, p2; rep from * to end.

2nd row: K2, *yf, k2togtbl, p1, k2; rep from * to end.

Rep these 2 rows.

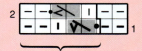

Rep these 5 sts

Cable Panels

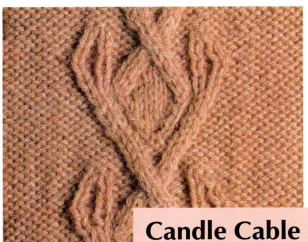

Candle Cable

Panel of 18 sts on a background of reverse st st.

1st row (right side): P1, T2F, k1, p3, C4F, p3, k1, T2B, p1.
2nd row: K7, p4, k7.
3rd row: P6, T3B, T3F, p6.
4th row: K6, p2, k2, p2, k6.
5th row: P5, T3B, p2, T3F, p5.
6th row: K5, p8, k5.
7th row: P4, C3B, C2B, C2F, C3F, p4.
8th row: K4, p10, k4.
9th row: P3, C3B, C2B, k2, C2F, C3F, p3.
10th row: K3, p12, k3.
11th row: P2, C3B, C2B, k4, C2F, C3F, p2.
12th row: K2, p14, k2.
13th row: P1, T2B, k1, T3F, k4, T3B, k1, T2F, p1.
14th row: K1, [p1, k1] twice, p8, [k1, p1] twice, k1.
15th row: T2B, p1, k1, p1, T3F, k2, T3B, p1, k1, p1, T2F.
16th row: [P1, k2] twice, p6, [k2, p1] twice.
17th row: T2F, p1, k1, p2, T3F, T3B, p2, k1, p1, T2B.
18th row: [K1, p1] twice, k3, p4, k3, [p1, k1] twice.

Rep these 18 rows.

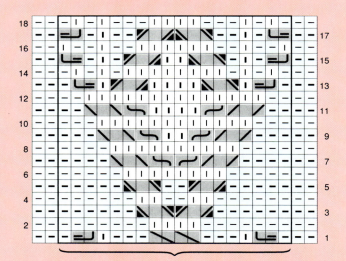

Panel of 18 sts

Cable Panels

Celtic Plait

Multiple of 10 sts + 15. The example shown is worked over 25 sts on a background of reverse st st.

Foundation row 1: K3, *p4, k6; rep from * to last 2 sts, p2.

Foundation row 2: K2, *p6, k4; rep from * to last 3 sts, p3.

1st row (right side): K3, *p4, C6F; rep from * to last 2 sts, p2.

2nd row: K2, *p6, k4; rep from * to last 3 sts, p3.

3rd row: *T5L, T5R; rep from * to last 5 sts, T5L.

4th row: P3, *k4, p6; rep from * to last 2 sts, k2.

5th row: P2, *C6B, p4; rep from * to last 3 sts, k3.

6th row: As 4th row.

7th row: *T5R, T5L; rep from * to last 5 sts, T5R.

8th row: As 2nd row.

Rep these 8 rows.

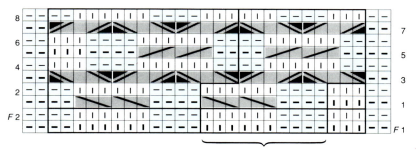

Rep these 10 sts

For abbreviations and chart symbols see pages 19 and 20.

Cable Panels

Fishernet Pattern

Multiple of 8 sts + 8. The example shown is worked over 24 sts on a background of reverse st st.

1st row (right side): P1, *T3F, T3B, p2; rep from * to 7 sts before end of panel, T3F, T3B, p1.

2nd row: K2, *p4, k4; rep from * to 6 sts before end of panel, p4, k2.

3rd row: P2, *C4F, p4; rep from * to 6 sts before end of panel, C4F, p2.

4th row: As 2nd row.

5th row: P1, *T3B, T3F, p2; rep from * to 7 sts before end of panel, T3B, T3F, p1.

6th row: K1, *p2, k2; rep from * to 3 sts before end of panel, p2, k1.

7th to 12th rows: Rep these 6 rows once more.

13th row: *T3B, p2, T3F; rep from * to end of panel.

14th row: P2, *k4, p4; rep from * to 6 sts before end of panel, k4, p2.

15th row: K2, *p4, C4B; rep from * to 6 sts before end of panel, p4, k2.

16th row: As 14th row.

17th row: K2, p3, *T3B, T3F, p2; rep from * to 3 sts before end of panel, p1, k2.

18th row: P2, k3, *p2, k2; rep from * to 3 sts before end of panel, k1, p2.

19th row: K2, p3, *T3F, T3B, p2; rep from * to 3 sts before end of panel, p1, k2.

20th to 22nd rows: Rep 14th and 15th rows once, then 14th row again.

23rd row: *T3F, p2, T3B; rep from * to end of panel.

24th row: As 6th row.

Rep these 24 rows.

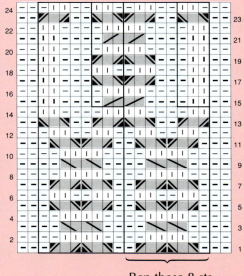

Rep these 8 sts

Cable Panels

Criss-Cross Cable with Twists

Panel of 16 sts on a background of reverse st st.

1st row (right side): P2, C4F, p4, C4F, p2.
2nd row: K2, p4, k4, p4, k2.
3rd row: P2, k4, p4, k4, p2.
4th row: As 2nd row.
5th and 6th rows: As 1st and 2nd rows.
7th row: [T4B, T4F] twice.
8th row: P2, k4, p4, k4, p2.
9th row: K2, p4, C4F, p4, k2.
10th row: As 8th row.
11th row: K2, p4, k4, p4, k2.
12th row: As 8th row.
13th row: As 9th row.
14th to 21st rows: Rep the last 4 rows twice more.
22nd row: As 8th row.
23rd row: [T4F, T4B] twice.
24th row: As 2nd row.
Rep these 24 rows.

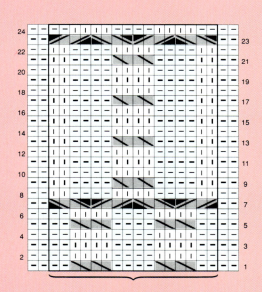

Panel of 16 sts

Cable Panels

Tramline Cable

Panel of 18 sts on a background of reverse st st.

1st row (right side): K2, p3, k2, p4, k2, p3, k2.

2nd row: P2, k3, p2, k4, p2, k3, p2.

3rd and 4th rows: Rep these 2 rows once more.

5th row: [T3F, p2] twice, T3B, p2, T3B.

6th row: K1, p2, k3, p2, k2, p2, k3, p2, k1.

7th row: P1, T3F, p2, T3F, T3B, p2, T3B, p1.

8th row: K2, p2, k3, p4, k3, p2, k2.

9th row: P2, T3F, p2, C4B, p2, T3B, p2.

10th row: K3, p2, k2, p4, k2, p2, k3.

11th row: P3, [T3F, T3B] twice, p3.

12th row: K4, p4, k2, p4, k4.

13th row: P4, C4F, p2, C4F, p4.

14th row: As 12th row.

15th row: P3, [T3B, T3F] twice, p3.

16th row: As 10th row.

17th row: P2, T3B, p2, C4B, p2, T3F, p2.

18th row: As 8th row.

19th row: P1, T3B, p2, T3B, T3F, p2, T3F, p1.

20th row: As 6th row.

21st row: [T3B, p2] twice, T3F, p2, T3F.

22nd row: As 2nd row.

23rd to 26th rows: Rep 1st and 2nd rows twice.

Rep these 26 rows.

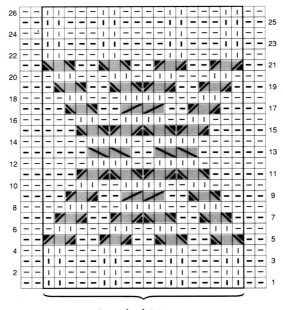

Panel of 18 sts

Cable Panels

Noughts and Crosses Cable

Panel of 12 sts on a background of reverse st st.

1st row (right side): K12.
2nd row: P12.
3rd and 4th rows: Rep these 2 rows once more.
5th row: C6B, C6F.
6th row: P12.
7th to 12th rows: Rep these 6 rows once more.
13th to 16th rows: Rep 1st and 2nd rows twice.
17th row: C6F, C6B.
18th row: P12.
19th to 24th rows: Rep the last 6 rows once more.

Rep these 24 rows.

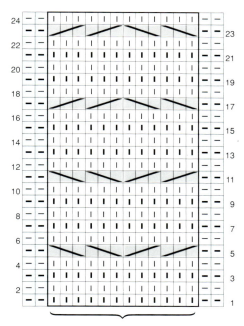

Panel of 12 sts

All-over Cable Patterns

Woven Lattice Pattern

Multiple of 6 sts + 8.

1st row (wrong side): K3, p4, *k2, p4; rep from * to last st, k1.

2nd row: P1, C4F, *p2, C4F; rep from * to last 3 sts, p3.

3rd row: As 1st row.

4th row: P3, *k2, T4B; rep from * to last 5 sts, k4, p1.

5th row: K1, p4, *k2, p4; rep from * to last 3 sts, k3.

6th row: P3, C4B, *p2, C4B; rep from * to last st, p1.

7th row: As 5th row.

8th row: P1, k4, *T4F, k2; rep from * to last 3 sts, p3.

Rep these 8 rows.

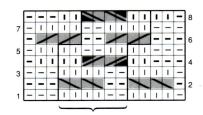

Rep these 6 sts

Cable Fabric

Multiple of 6 sts + 8.

1st row (right side): Knit.

2nd row: Purl.

3rd row: K3, C4B, *k2, C4B; rep from * to last st, k1.

4th row: Purl.

5th and 6th rows: As 1st and 2nd rows.

7th row: K1, *C4F, k2; rep from * to last st, k1.

8th row: Purl.

Rep these 8 rows.

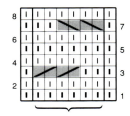

Rep these 6 sts

All-over Cable Patterns

Cable and Eyelet Rib

Multiple of 7 sts + 3.

1st row (right side): P3, *k4, p3; rep from * to end.

2nd row: K1, yf, k2tog, *p4, k1, yf, k2tog; rep from * to end.

3rd row: P3, *C4B, p3; rep from * to end.

4th row: As 2nd row.

5th and 6th rows: As 1st and 2nd rows.

Rep these 6 rows.

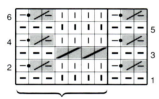

Rep these 7 sts

Eyelet Cable

Multiple of 8 sts + 1.

Special Abbreviation

 C3Rtog (Cross 3 Right together) = slip next 2 sts on to cable needle and hold at back of work, knit next st from left-hand needle, then k2tog from cable needle.

1st row (right side): P1, *C3Rtog, p1, k3, p1; rep from * to end.

2nd row: K1, *p3, k1, p1, yrn, p1, k1; rep from * to end.

3rd row: P1, *k3, p1, C3Rtog, p1; rep from * to end.

4th row: K1, *p1, yrn, p1, k1, p3, k1; rep from * to end.

Rep these 4 rows.

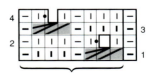

Rep these 8 sts

Cable Patterns

Ridge and Cable Stripes

Multiple of 10 sts + 8.

1st row (right side): Knit.

2nd row: Purl.

3rd and 4th rows: Rep these 2 rows once more.

5th row: K7, *C4B, k6; rep from * to last st, k1.

6th row: K7, *p4, k6; rep from * to last st, k1.

7th row: P7, *k4, p6; rep from * to last st, p1.

8th row: As 6th row.

9th row: P7, *C4B, p6; rep from * to last st, p1.

10th to 12 rows: Rep 6th and 7th rows once, then 6th row again.

13th row: As 5th row.

14th row: Purl.

15th to 18th rows: Rep 1st and 2nd rows twice.

19th row: K2, C4F, *k6, C4F; rep from * to last 2 sts, k2.

20th row: K2, p4, *k6, p4; rep from * to last 2 sts, k2.

21st row: P2, k4, *p6, k4; rep from * to last 2 sts, p2.

22nd row: As 20th row.

23rd row: P2, C4F, *p6, C4F; rep from * to last 2 sts, p2.

24th to 26th rows: Rep 20th and 21st rows once, then 20th row again.

27th row: As 19th row.

28th row: Purl.

Rep these 28 rows.

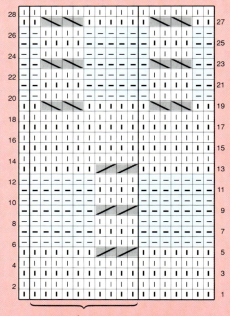

Rep these 10 sts

Man's Cardigan

Measurements

To fit chest size	85/90	95/100	105/110	cm
	34/36	38/40	42/44	ins
Finished measurement	103	114	124	cm
	41	45½	49½	ins
Length to shoulder	66	70	72	cm
(approximately)	26	27¾	28¼	ins
Sleeve length	46	47	48	cm
(approximately)	18	18½	19	ins

Shown in 105/110 cm [42/44 inch] size.

Materials

Double Knitting yarn

Colour A	250	275	300	grams
	9	10	11	ounces
Colour B	200	225	225	grams
	8	9	9	ounces
Colour C	175	200	200	grams
	7	8	8	ounces
Colour D	175	200	200	grams
	7	8	8	ounces

Pair needles each size 4mm (UK 8, USA 6) and 3¼mm (UK 10, USA 3 or 4). 8 buttons.

The quantities of yarn stated are based on average requirements and are therefore approximate.

For abbreviations see pages 19 and 20.

Tension

22 sts and 30 rows = 10 cm [4 ins] square measured over st st using larger needles.

Back

Using smaller needles and A cast on 97(107-119) sts.

1st row (right side): K1, *p1, k1; rep from * to end.

2nd row: P1, *k1, p1; rep from * to end.

Rep the last 2 rows 11 times more, then 1st row again.

Next row (increase): Rib 3(2-8), *inc in next st, rib 5(5-5); rep from * to last 4(3-9) sts, inc in next st, rib to end. 113(125-137) sts.

Change to larger needles and following chart for Back work in st st starting knit, until the 106th(112th-112th) row has been worked, thus ending with a purl row.

Shape Armholes

Cast off 4(5-5) sts at beg of next 2 rows. Dec 1 st at each end of next 3(5-5) rows, then following 5(4-6) alt rows. 89(97-105) sts remain. Work straight until the 176th(188th-194th) row has been worked, thus ending with a purl row.

Shape Shoulders

Cast off 9(10-11) sts at beg of next 4 rows, then 10(11-12) sts at beg of following 2 rows. Cast off remaining 33(35-37) sts.

Left Front

Using smaller needles and A cast on 55(61-67) sts and work 4 rows in k1, p1 rib as given for Back.

Next row (buttonhole): Rib to last 7 sts, cast off next 2 sts, rib to end.

Work 17 more rows in rib casting on 2 sts over buttonhole in first of these rows, then work buttonhole row again. Work 2 more rows in rib casting on 2 sts over buttonhole in first of these rows.

Next row: Rib 10, slip these sts on to a safety pin for front band, rib 1(4-3), *inc in next st, rib 5(5-6); rep from * to last 2(5-5) sts, inc in next st, rib to end. 53(59-65) sts.

Change to larger needles and following chart for Left Front work in st st starting knit, until front is 10 rows shorter than back to start of armhole shaping, thus ending with a purl row.

Shape Front Slope

1st row: Knit to last 3 sts, k2tog, k1. (1 st decreased at front edge).

★★ Work 3 rows straight. Dec 1 st at front edge as before on next and following 4th row. 50(56-62) sts remain. Purl 1 row. (Work 1 row more here for right front).

Shape Armhole

Cast off 4(5-5) sts at beg of next row. Purl 1 row (omit this row for right front).

Continuing to dec 1 st at front edge as before on next and every following 6th row, **at the same time** dec 1 st at armhole edge on next 3(5-5) rows, then on following 5(4-6) alt rows. 35(39-43) sts remain. Keeping armhole edge straight continue to dec 1 st at front edge on every 6th row from last dec until 28(31-34) sts remain. Work straight until front measures same as back to start of shoulder shaping, ending at armhole edge.

Shape Shoulder

Cast off 9(10-11) sts at beg of next and following alt row. Work 1 row. Cast off remaining 10(11-12) sts.

Right Front

Using smaller needles and A cast on 55(61-67) sts and work 25 rows in k1, p1 rib as given for Back.

Next row: Rib 1(4-3), *inc in next st, rib 5(5-6); rep from * to last 12(15-15) sts, inc in next st, rib 1(4-4), turn and slip remaining 10 sts on to a safety pin for front band. 53(59-65) sts.

Change to larger needles and following chart for Right Front work in st st starting knit, until front is 10 rows shorter than back to start of armhole shaping, thus ending with a purl row.

Shape Front Slope

1st row: K1, sl 1, k1, psso, knit to end. (1 st decreased at front edge). Complete to match Left Front from ★★ to end, reversing shapings by working 1 row more and 1 row less where indicated.

Man's Cardigan

Sleeves

Using smaller needles and A cast on 53(57-61) sts and work 6 cm [2½ ins] in k1, p1 rib as given for Back ending with a right side row.

Next row (increase): Rib 6(2-4), *inc in next st, rib 2(3-3); rep from * to last 8(3-5) sts, inc in next st, rib to end. 67(71-75) sts.

Change to larger needles and following chart for Sleeves work 4 rows in st st starting knit. Inc 1 st at each end of next and every following 7th(6th-6th) row until there are 89(103-99) sts, then every following 6th(5th-5th) row until there are 101(111-119) sts. Work 11 rows straight, thus ending with the 120th(124th-126th) row of chart.

Shape Top

Cast off 4(5-5) sts at beg of next 2 rows. Dec 1 st at each end of next and every alt row until 81(87-91) sts remain. Purl 1 row. Cast off 5(4-4) sts at beg of next 10(14-14) rows. Cast off remaining 31(31-35) sts.

Finishing and Front Bands

Block or press pieces according to instructions on ball band. Join shoulder seams.

Right Front Band

Using smaller needles and A cast on 1 st and with wrong side of right front facing, rib across sts on safety pin. 11 sts. Continue in rib until band **when slightly stretched** fits up front and round to centre back neck. Cast off in rib.

Sew band in place stretching evenly and mark positions for 8 buttons, the first two to match existing buttonholes in left front welt and the top one to be 1 cm [½ inch] below start of front slope shaping. Space remainder evenly between.

Left Front Band

Work as given for Right Front Band but starting with right side of left front facing and **at the same time** making buttonholes to match markers on right side rows as before.

Sew band in place and join at centre back. Join side and sleeve seams. Insert sleeves. Sew on buttons.

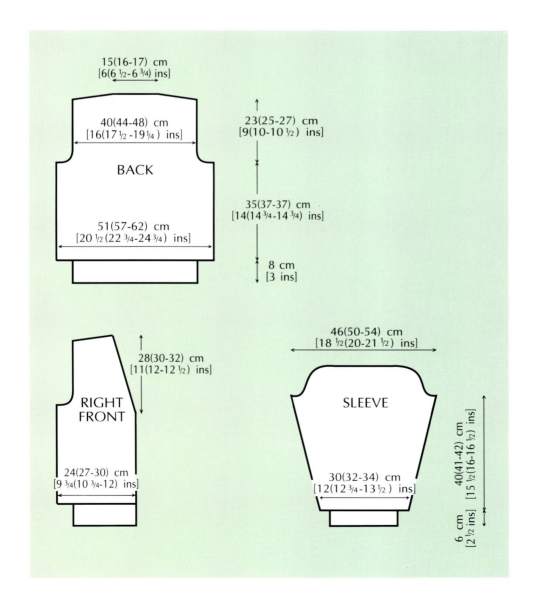

Man's Cardigan

Back and Front

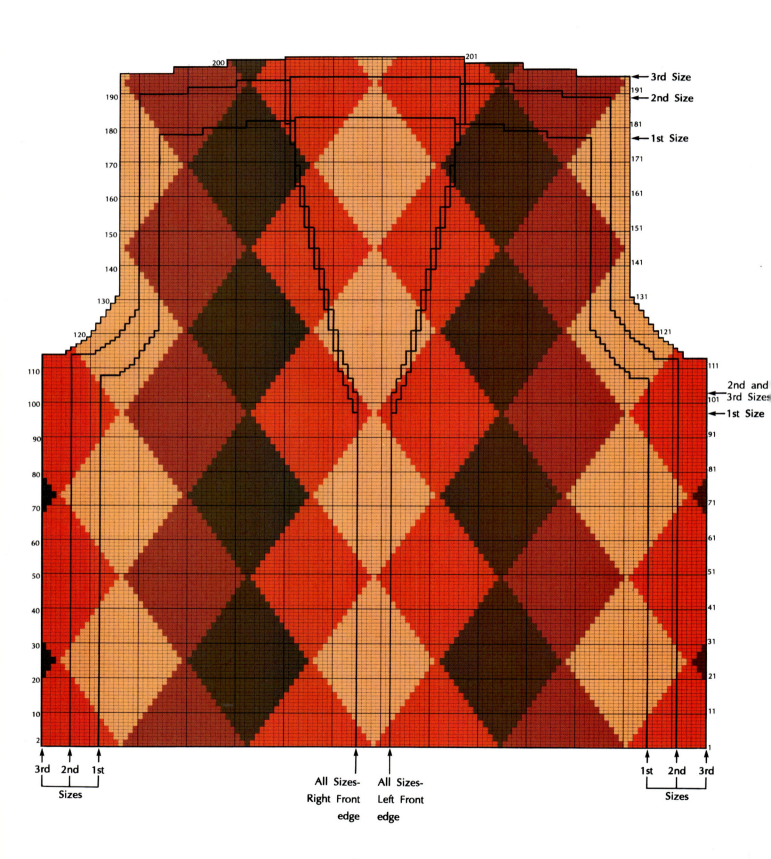

Man's Cardigan

Sleeve

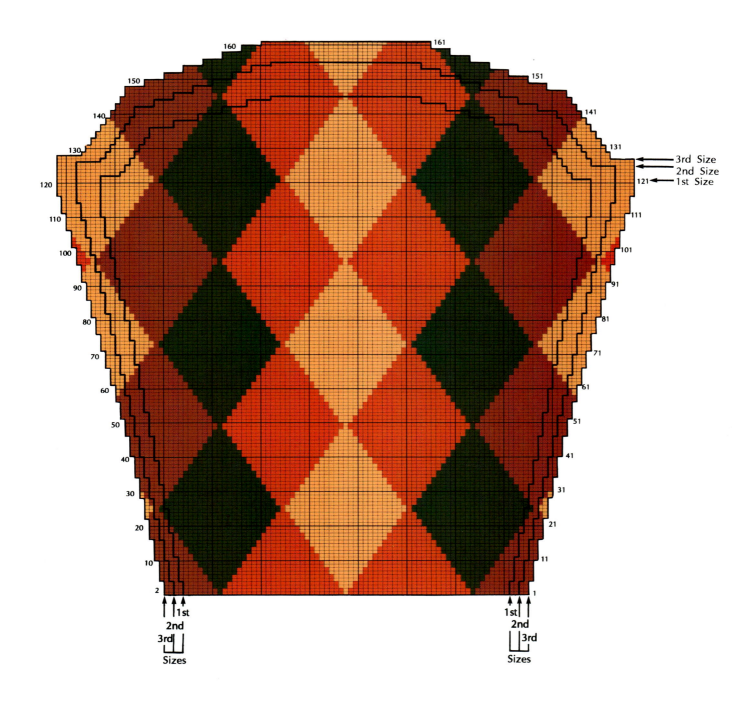

Note: Follow intarsia chart using a separate length of yarn for each colour block. Do not carry yarns across the wrong side of work. Work to the colour change, then making sure both yarns are at the wrong side of the work, drop the first colour, pick up the second colour and bring it around the first colour to cross the yarns over before working the next stitch.

Row numbers are shown at the sides of the chart at the beginning of the row. Right side rows (odd numbers) are always read from right to left. Wrong side rows (even numbers) are always read from left to right. Read the chart exactly as the knitting is worked - from the bottom to the top.

Intarsia Motifs

Bird of Paradise Chart

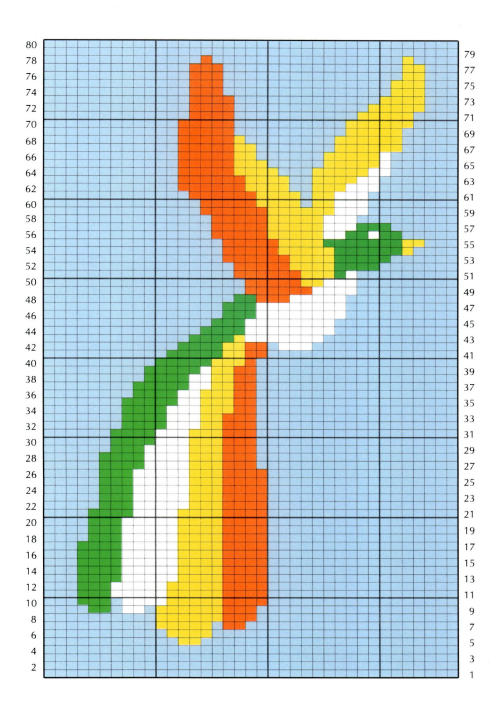

Intarsia Motifs

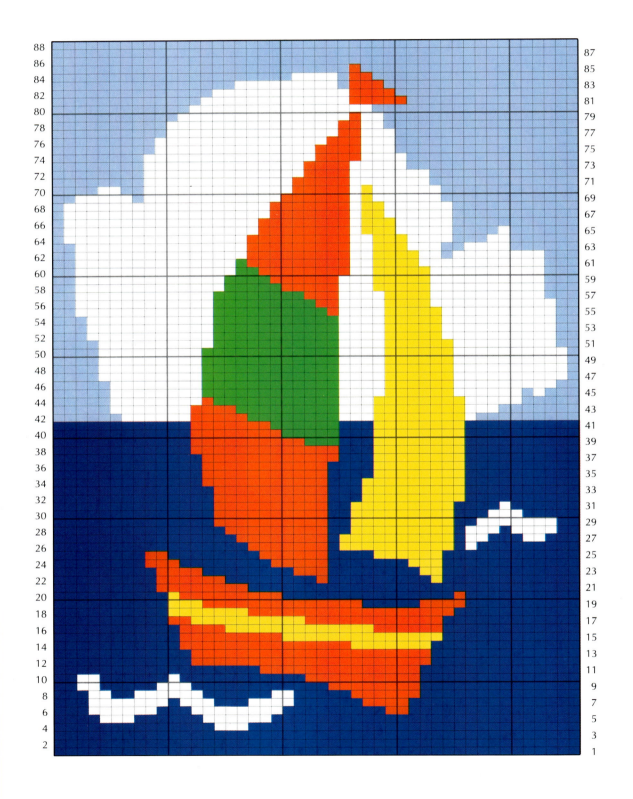

Sail Away Chart

Intarsia Motifs

Fruit Cocktail Chart

Fair Isle Top

Measurements

To fit bust size	80/85	90/95	100/105	cm
	32/34	36/38	40/42	ins
Finished measurement	103	119	135	cm
	41	47	54	ins
Length to shoulder	58	59	60	cm
(approximately)	23	23½	24	ins
Sleeve length	28	28	28	cm
(approximately)	11	11	11	ins

Shown in 90/95 cm [36/38 inch] size.

Materials

Double Knitting yarn

Main Colour (M)	450	500	600	grams
(pale blue)	16	18	22	ounces
Contrast Colour A	100	100	100	grams
(pale pink)	4	4	4	ounces
Contrast Colour B	100	150	150	grams
(sand)	4	6	6	ounces
Contrast Colour C	50	100	100	grams
(white)	2	4	4	ounces
Contrast Colour D	50	50	50	grams
(coral)	2	2	2	ounces

Pair needles each size 3¼mm (UK 10, USA 3 or 4), 4mm (UK 8, USA 6) and 4½mm (UK 7, USA 7).
Cable needle.

The quantities of yarn stated are based on average requirements and are therefore approximate.
For abbreviations see pages 19 and 20.

Tension

22 sts and 30 rows = 10 cm [4 ins] square measured over st st using middle size needles.

Special Abbreviation

C12F (Cable 12 Front) = slip next 6 sts on to cable needle and hold at front of work, knit next 6 sts from left-hand needle, then knit sts from cable needle.

Note: Do not weave yarn in at back of work. Carry colour not in use **loosely** across back of work twisting yarns together at each colour change to avoid making a hole.

Charts 1 and 3: Read odd number (knit) rows from right to left and even number (purl) rows from left to right.

Chart 2: Read odd number (purl) rows from left to right and even number (knit) rows from right to left.

Back

Using middle size needles and M, cast on 113(131-149) sts, and starting knit, work 14(18-20) rows in st st, thus ending with a purl row.

Commence pattern.

★**Next row:** K1, *k2tog, yf, k1; rep from * to last st, k1.

Next row: Purl.

★★Change to largest needles and, joining in and breaking off colours as required, work the 9 rows of chart 1, thus ending with a knit row. ★★★

Change to middle size needles and working in M only, continue as follows:

Next row: Purl.

Next row: K1, *k2tog, yf, k1; rep from * to last st, k1. ★★★★

Starting purl, work 19 rows in st st, thus ending with a purl row.

Rep from ★ to ★★★.

Joining in and breaking off colours as required, work the 25 rows of chart 2, thus ending with a purl row.

Rep from ★★ to ★★★★.

Starting purl, work 19 rows in st st, thus ending with a purl row.

Rep from ★ to ★★★★.

Starting purl, work 25(25-27) rows in st st, thus ending with a purl row.

Shape Shoulders

Cast off 18(23-26) sts at beg of next 2 rows, then 19(23-26) sts at beg of following 2 rows. Slip remaining 39(39-45) sts on to a holder.

Front

Work as given for Back until front is 22(22-24) rows shorter than back to start of shoulder shaping, thus ending with a purl row.

Shape Neck

Next row: K47(56-63), turn and complete this side first.

Dec 1 st at neck edge on next 4(4-8) rows, then on following 6(6-3) alt rows. 37(46-52) sts remain. Work 5(5-9) rows straight (work 1 row more here for 2nd side), thus ending at side edge.

Shape Shoulder

Cast off 18(23-26) sts at beg of next row. Work 1 row. Cast off remaining 19(23-26) sts.

With right side of work facing, slip centre 19(19-23) sts on to a holder, rejoin M to remaining 47(56-53) sts, knit to end. Complete to match first side, reversing shapings by working 1 row more where indicated.

Sleeves

Using smallest needles and M, cast on 63(67-75) sts.

1st row (right side): K1, *p1, k1; rep from * to end.

2nd row: P1, *k1, p1; rep from * to end.

Rep the last 2 rows until rib measures 5 cm [2 ins], ending with a right side row.

Next row (increase): Rib 5(3-4), *inc in next st, rib 3(3-5); rep from * to last 6(4-5) sts, inc in next st, rib to end. 77(83-87) sts.

Change to middle size needles and starting knit, work 6 rows in st st, increasing 1 st at each end of 3rd row. 79(85-89) sts.

Fair Isle Top

Next row: Inc in first st, k1(1-0), k2tog, yf, *k1, k2tog, yf; rep from * to last 3(3-2) sts, k1(1-0), inc in next st, k1. 81(87-91) sts.

Next row: Purl.

Change to largest needles and, joining in and breaking off colours as required, work the 43 rows of chart 3, increasing 1 st at each end of 3rd and every following 4th row as indicated until there are 103(109-113) sts.

Change to middle size needles and continue in M only.

Next row: Purl.

Next row: K2(2-1), *k2tog, yf, k1; rep from * to last 2(2-1) sts, k2(2-1).

Next row: Purl.

Knit 1 row increasing 1 st at each end of next row. 105(111-115) sts. Continuing in st st, work 5 rows straight, thus ending with a purl row. Cast off **loosely**.

Finishing and Edgings

Block, but do not press.

Join right shoulder seam.

Neckband

With right side facing, using smallest needles and M, pick up and k24(24-26) sts down left front slope, knit across sts on holder at front neck, pick up and k24(24-26) sts up right front slope, then knit across sts on holder at back neck decreasing 1 st at centre. 105(105-119) sts.

Starting with a 2nd row, work 3 cm [1¼ ins] in k1, p1 rib as given for Sleeves. Cast off in rib.

Join left shoulder seam and ends of neckband. Fold each sleeve in half lengthways and mark centre of cast off edge. Sew each sleeve to a side edge, placing centre at shoulder seam. Join side and sleeve seams.

Lower Border

Using middle size needles and M, cast on 13 sts and commence pattern.

1st row (right side): Knit.

2nd row: P12, k1.

3rd to 6th rows: Rep 1st and 2nd rows twice more.

7th row: K1, C12F.

8th row: As 2nd row.

9th to 16th rows: Rep 1st and 2nd rows 4 times.

These 16 rows form the pattern. Continue in pattern until strip fits from left side seam all round lower edge. Sew in place as illustrated. Join border edges.

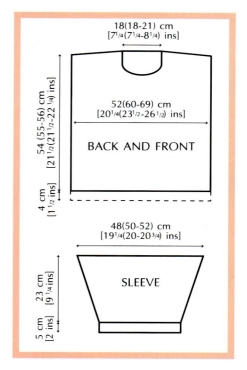

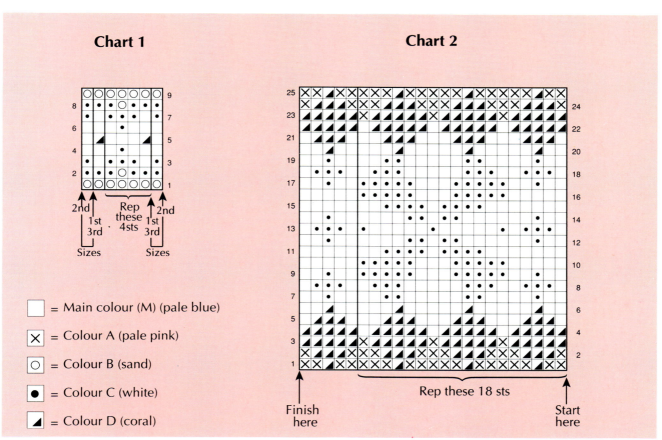

Fair Isle Top

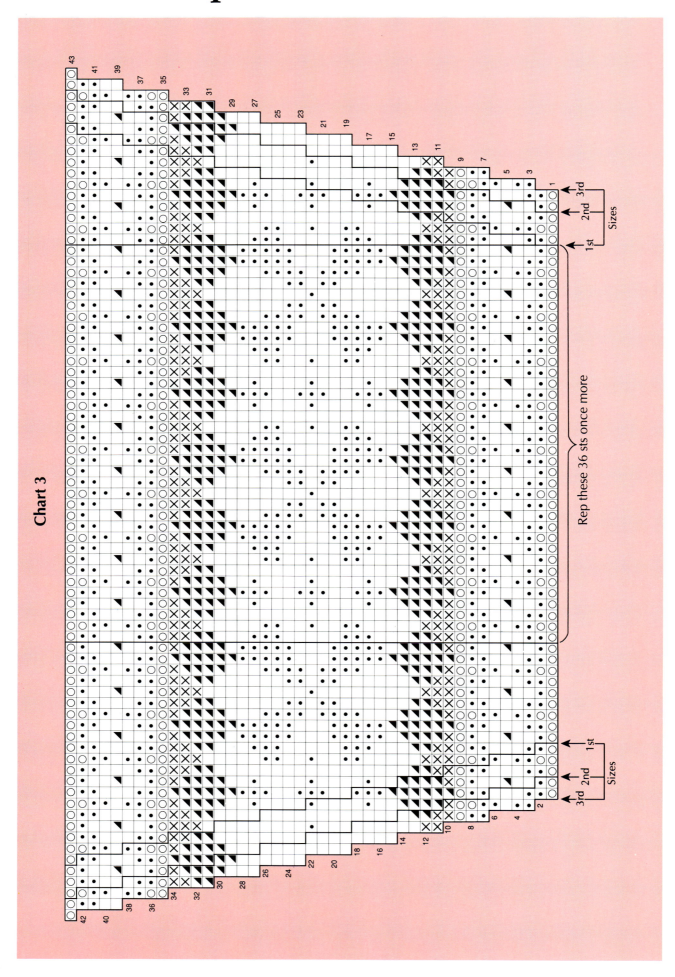

Fair Isle Patterns

Honeysuckle

Multiple of 24 sts + 1.

Rep rows 1 to 28.

3-Colour Pattern

□ = Colour A (green)

● = Colour B (red)

✕ = Colour C (yellow)

2-Colour Pattern

□ = Colour A (white)

●
✕ } = Colour B (blue)

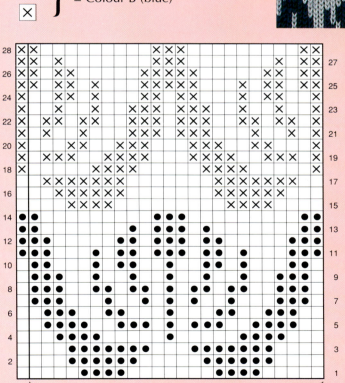

Rep these 24 sts

69

Fair Isle Patterns

2-Colour Checks

Multiple of 24 sts +1.
Rep rows 1 to 28.

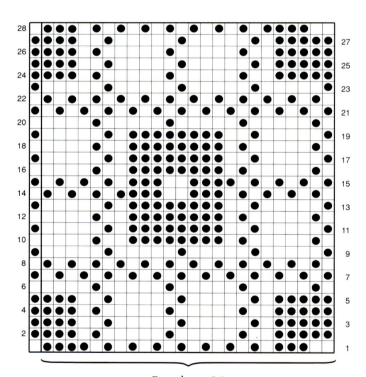

Rep these 24 sts

☐ = Colour A (cream)   ● = Colour B (dark green)

Fair Isle Patterns

Colour Pyramids

Multiple of 24 sts + 1.

Rep rows 1 to 8.

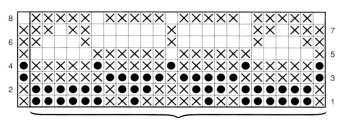

Rep these 24 sts

☐ = Colour A (yellow) ● = Colour B (mauve)
☒ = Colour C (cream)

Elephants

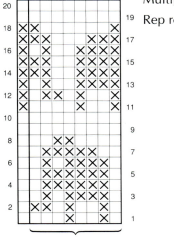

Multiple of 8 sts + 1.

Rep rows 1 to 20.

Rep these 8 sts

☐ = Main Colour M (light blue) ☒ = Contrast Colour C (red)

Fair Isle Patterns

Fair Isle Chevron

Multiple of 6 sts + 1.
Rep rows 1 to 36.

4-Colour Pattern

☐ = Colour A (yellow)

● = Colour B (green)

✗ = Colour C (blue)

○ = Colour D (red)

2-Colour Pattern

●
✗ } = Colour A (yellow)

☐
○ } = Colour B (blue)

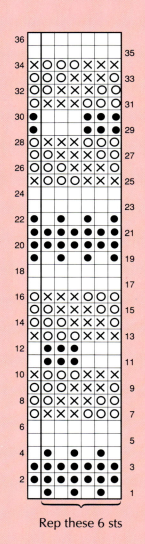

Rep these 6 sts

Fair Isle Patterns

Ducks

Multiple of 8 sts + 1.
Rep rows 1 to 28.

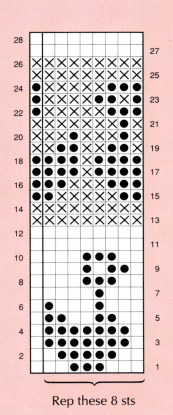

Rep these 8 sts

3-Colour Pattern

☐ = Colour A (turquoise)
● = Colour B (white)
✕ = Colour C (sea green)

2-Colour Pattern

☐ ⎫
✕ ⎬ = Colour A (blue)
● = Colour B (yellow)

Child's Sailor Cardigan

Measurements

To fit chest size	50	55	60	65	cm
	20	22	24	26	ins
Finished measurement	57	62	67	72	cm
	23	25	27	29	ins
Length to shoulder	28	32	37	42	cm
	11	12 3/4	14 1/2	16 1/2	ins
Sleeve length	20	24	28	32	cm
	8	9 1/2	11	12 1/2	ins

Shown in 65 cm [26 inch] size.

Materials

Double Knitting yarn

Main Colour (M)	150	200	200	250	grams
	6	8	8	9	ounces
Contrast Colour (C)	50	50	50	50	grams
	2	2	2	2	ounces

Pair needles each size 4mm (UK 8, USA 6) and 3 1/4mm (UK 10, USA 3 or 4).

4(5-6-6) buttons.

The quantities of yarn stated are based on average requirements and are therefore approximate.

For abbreviations see pages 19 and 20.

Tension

24 sts and 32 rows = 10 cm [4 ins] square measured over st st using larger needles.

Back

Using smaller needles and M, cast on 69(75-81-87) sts.

1st row (right side): K1, *p1, k1; rep from * to end.

2nd row: P1, *k1, p1; rep from * to end.

★ Join in C. Keeping rib correct work 2 rows in C, 4(4-6-6) rows in M, 2 rows in C then 4(4-6-6) rows in M ★.

Change to larger needles and using M, work 4 rows in st st, starting knit. Work the 6 rows of chart 1, then continue in M only until back measures 17(20-24-27) cm [6 3/4(8-9 1/2-10 1/2) ins] ending with a purl row.

Shape Armholes

Cast off 3(3-4-4) sts at beg of next 2 rows. Dec 1 st at each end of next 3 rows, then on following 2 alt rows. 53(59-63-69) sts remain. Work straight until armholes measure 11(12-13-15) cm [4 1/4(4 3/4-5-6) ins], measured straight from start of armhole shaping ending with a purl row.

Shape Shoulders

Cast off 5(6-6-7) sts at beg of next 4 rows, then 5(5-7-7) sts at beg of following 2 rows. Cast off remaining 23(25-25-27) sts.

Left Front

Using smaller needles and M, cast on 32(34-38-40) sts.

1st row (right side): *K1, p1; rep from * to last 2 sts, k2.

2nd row: P2, *k1, p1; rep from * to end.

Work as given for Back from ★ to ★.

★★ Change to larger needles and using M knit 1 row decreasing 1 st at centre of row for 1st(3rd) sizes only. 31(34-37-40) sts. Using M work 3 rows in st st, starting purl. Work the 6 rows of chart 2, then continue in M only until front is 6 rows shorter than back to start of armhole shaping thus ending with a purl row. Place a marker at beg(front edge) of last row.

Shape Front Slope

Dec 1 st at front edge of next and following 4th row. 29(32-35-38) sts remain. Work 1 row straight (work 1 row more here for right front) thus ending at side edge.

Shape Armhole

Cast off 3(3-4-4) sts at beg of next row. Work 1 row (omit this row for right front). Dec 1 st at front edge on next and following 4th row, **at the same time** dec 1 st at armhole edge on next 3 rows, then on following 2 alt rows. 19(22-24-27) sts remain. Work 1 row straight. Keeping armhole edge straight dec 1 st at front edge on next and every following 4th row until 17(18-22-25) sts remain, then every following 6th row until 15(17-19-21) sts remain.

Work straight until front measures same as back to start of shoulder shaping ending with a purl row (work 1 row more here for right front) thus ending at armhole edge.

Shape Shoulder

Cast off 5(6-6-7) sts at beg of next and following alt row. Work 1 row. Cast off remaining 5(5-7-7) sts.

Right Front

Using smaller needles and M, cast on 32(34-38-40) sts.

1st row (right side): K2, *p1, k1; rep from * to end.

2nd row: *P1, k1; rep from * to last 2 sts, p2.

Work as given for Back from ★ to ★.

Work to match Left Front from ★★ to end working chart 3 instead of chart 2 and reversing all shapings.

Sleeves

Using smaller needles and M, cast on 39(41-45-47) sts and work 14(14-18-18) rows in striped k1, p1 rib as given for Back. Break off C and continue in M only.

Change to larger needles and work 4 rows in st st, starting knit. Inc 1 st at each end of next and every following 6th(8th-9th-10th) row until there are 53(55-59-63) sts. Work straight until sleeve measures 20(24-28-32) cm [8(9 1/2-11-12 1/2) ins], or required length ending with a purl row.

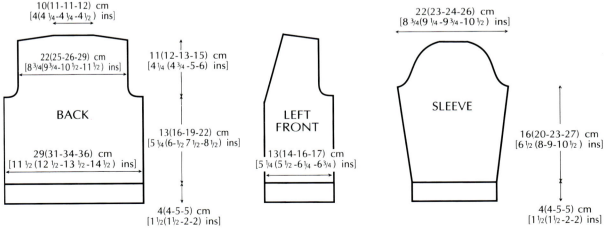

Child's Sailor Cardigan

Shape Top
Cast off 3(3-4-4) sts at beg of next 2 rows. Dec 1 st at each end of next 3 rows, then every alt row until 29(29-27-27) sts remain. Dec 1 st at each end of next 3 rows, then cast off 4 sts at beg of next 2 rows. Cast off remaining 15(15-13-13) sts.

Collar

Left Half
Using larger needles and M cast on 2 sts and work 2 rows in st st, starting knit. Inc 1 st at end of next and every following 6th(4th-4th-4th) row until there are 9(12-13-15) sts. Work straight until piece measures 15(16-17-19) cm [6(6 1/4-6 3/4-7 1/2) ins] along straight edge ending with a knit row (work 1 row more here for right half). Slip sts onto a holder.

Right Half
Work as given for Left Half reversing shaping by working incs at beg of rows instead of end and working 1 row more where indicated. Do not break yarn at end.

Back
Continuing on from sts of right half cast on 23(25-25-27) sts, turn and purl across sts of left half. 41(49-51-57) sts. Work straight until back collar measures 8(9-10-11) cm [3(3 1/2-4-4 1/4) ins] ending with a knit row. Change to smaller needles.

Next row (increase): P5(3-4-1), *inc in next st, p5; rep from * to last 6(4-5-2) sts, inc in next st, purl to end. 47(57-59-67) sts. Tie a marker at each end of row.

Work 2 rows in k1, p1 rib as given for Back. Keeping rib correct work 1 more row in M, 2 rows in C, then 4 rows in M, **at the same time** inc 1 st at each end of next and following alt row, then on following 4 rows. 59(69-71-79) sts. Using M cast off in rib.

Finishing and Edgings
Block or press according to instructions on ball band.

Left Front Band
Using smaller needles and M, with right side of work facing, and starting at marker, pick up and k42(52-64-70) sts evenly along front edge.

Next row (wrong side): *P1, k1; rep from * to end.

Work 2 more rows in rib as set. Join in C.

Boy's Jacket Only
Next row (buttonholes): Using C, rib 3(3-3-4), [cast off next 2 sts in rib, rib until there are 9(9-9-10) sts on right-hand needle after casting off] 3(4-5-5) times, cast off next 2 sts, rib to end.

Using C work 1 row casting on 2 sts over each buttonhole.

Girl's Jacket only
Using C work 2 more rows in rib.

Girl's and Boy's Jacket
Break off C and continuing in M only work 4 more rows. Cast off in rib.

Right Front Band
Pick up and knit sts as given for Left Front Band but starting at lower edge and finishing at marker.

Next row (right side): *K1, p1; rep from * to end.

Work 2 more rows in rib as set. Join in C.

Girl's Jacket only
Next row (buttonholes): Using C, rib 4(3-4-4), [cast off next 2 sts in rib, rib until there are 9(9-9-10) sts on right-hand needle after casting off] 3(4-5-5) times, cast off next 2 sts, rib to end.

Using C work 1 row casting on 2 sts over each buttonhole.

Boy's Jacket Only
Using C work 2 more rows in rib.

Girl's and Boy's Jacket
Break off C and continuing in M only work 4 more rows. Cast off in rib.

Collar Edging
Using smaller needles and M, with right side of work facing and starting at cast on edge of left half, pick up and k65(71-75-85) sts evenly along side edge of collar to marker.

1st row: P1, *k1, p1; rep from * to end.

Keeping rib correct work 2 rows in M, 2 rows in C and 4 rows in M, **at the same time** increasing 1 st at back edge of following 2 alt rows then next 4 rows. 71(77-81-91) sts. Using M cast off in rib.

Work 2nd side to match but starting at marker at back edge of collar on right half.

Join shoulder, side and sleeve seams. Insert sleeves. Sew collar to neck edge. Join ends of bands. Press seams. Sew on buttons.

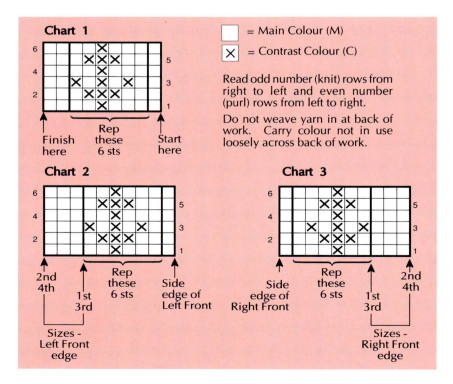

KNITTING stylish STITCHES

In the introduction section of this book we have talked about increasing and decreasing - essential for working the garment patterns. These techniques can also be used in pattern stitches to create `Rich Textures'. Raised Stitches can be achieved by working into the back of stitches.

Rich Textures

Foxgloves

Cast on a multiple of 10 sts + 16.

Note: Only count sts after 10th row of pattern.

1st row (right side): P6, *yon, k1, p2, k1, yfrn, p6; rep from * to end.

2nd row: P6, *yrn, p2, k2, p2, yrn, p6; rep from * to end.

3rd row: P6, *yon, k3, p2, k3, yfrn, p6; rep from * to end.

4th row: P6, *yrn, p4, k2, p4, yrn, p6; rep from * to end.

5th row: P6, *k5, p2, k5, p6; rep from * to end.

6th row: P11, *k2, p16; rep from * to last 13 sts, k2, p11.

7th row: P6, *sl 1, k1, psso, k3, p2, k3, k2tog, p6; rep from * to end.

8th row: P6, *p2tog, p2, k2, p2, p2togtbl, p6; rep from * to end.

9th row: P6, *sl 1, k1, psso, k1, p2, k1, k2tog, p6; rep from * to end.

10th row: P6, *p2tog, k2, p2togtbl, p6; rep from * to end.

Rep these 10 rows.

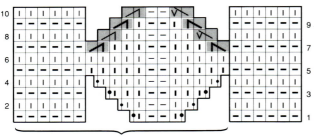

Little Fountain Pattern

Cast on a multiple of 4 sts + 5.

Note: Only count sts after 3rd and 4th rows.

1st row (right side): K1, *yf, k3, yf, k1; rep from * to end.

2nd row: Purl.

3rd row: K2, sl 1, k2tog, psso, *k3, sl 1, k2tog, psso; rep from * to last 2 sts, k2.

4th row: Purl.

Rep these 4 rows.

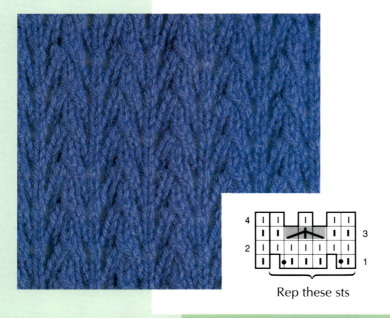

Rich Textures

Bud Stitch

Cast on a multiple of 6 sts + 5.

Note: Only count sts after 6th and 12th rows.

1st row (right side): P5, *k1, yfrn, p5; rep from * to end.

2nd row: K5, *p2, k5; rep from * to end.

3rd row: P5, *k2, p5; rep from * to end.

4th and 5th rows: Rep the last 2 rows once more.

6th row: K5, *p2tog, k5; rep from * to end.

7th row: P2, *k1, yfrn, p5; rep from * to last 3 sts, k1, yfrn, p2.

8th row: K2, *p2, k5; rep from * to last 4 sts, p2, k2.

9th row: P2, *k2, p5; rep from * to last 4 sts, k2, p2.

10th and 11th rows: Rep the last 2 rows once more.

12th row: K2, *p2tog, k5; rep from * to last 4 sts, p2tog, k2.

Rep these 12 rows.

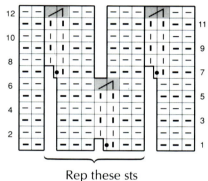

Open Check Stitch

Multiple of 2 sts + 2.

1st row (right side): Purl.

2nd row: Knit.

3rd row: K2, *sl 1, k1; rep from * to end.

4th row: *K1, sl 1; rep from * to last 2 sts, k2.

5th row: K1, *yf, k2tog; rep from * to last st, k1.

6th row: Purl.

Rep these 6 rows.

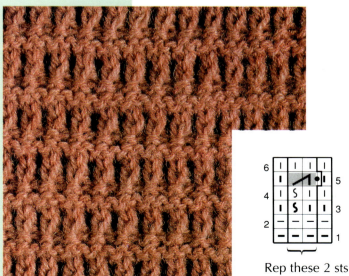

Raised Stitches

Crosses

Multiple of 12 sts + 13.

1st row (right side): Purl.

2nd row: Knit.

3rd row: P5, *[KB1] 3 times, p9; rep from * to last 8 sts, [KB1] 3 times, p5.

4th row: K5, *p3, k9; rep from * to last 8 sts, p3, k5.

5th and 6th rows: Rep the last 2 rows once more.

7th row: P2, *[KB1] 9 times, p3; rep from * to last 11 sts, [KB1] 9 times, p2.

8th row: K2, *p9, k3; rep from * to last 11 sts, p9, k2.

9th and 10th rows: Rep the last 2 rows once more.

11th to 14th rows: Rep 3rd and 4th rows twice.

15th and 16th rows: As 1st and 2nd rows.

Rep these 16 rows.

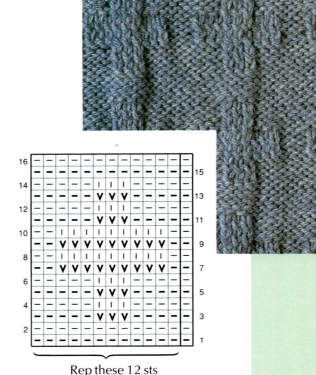

Embossed Lozenge Stitch

Multiple of 8 sts + 9.

1st row (right side): P3, *KB1, p1, KB1, p5; rep from * to last 6 sts, KB1, p1, KB1, p3.

2nd row: K3, *PB1, k1, PB1, k5; rep from * to last 6 sts, PB1, k1, PB1, k3.

3rd and 4th rows: Rep these 2 rows once more.

5th row: P2, *KB1, p3; rep from * to last 3 sts, KB1, p2.

6th row: K2, *PB1, k3; rep from * to last 3 sts, PB1, k2.

7th row: P1, *KB1, p5, KB1, p1; rep from * to end.

8th row: K1, *PB1, k5, PB1, k1; rep from * to end.

9th and 10th rows: Rep the last 2 rows once more.

11th and 12th rows: As 5th and 6th rows.

Rep these 12 rows.